Reconstructing Jury Instructions in Homicide Offenses

Rethinking Homicide Law

Hisham M. Ramadan

University Press of America,® Inc.
Dallas · Lanham · Boulder · New York · Oxford

4501 Forbes Boulevard
Suite 200
Lanham, Maryland 20706
UPA Acquisitions Department (301) 459-3366

PO Box 317
Oxford
OX2 9RU, UK

Printed in the United States of America
British Library Cataloging in Publication Information Available

Library of Congress Control Number: 2004102955
ISBN 0-7618-2853-2 (paperback : alk. ppr.)
ISBN 978-0-7618-2853-2

The paper used in this publication meets the minimum requirements of American National Standard for Information Sciences—Permanence of Paper for Printed Library Materials, ANSI Z39.48—1984

Dedication

To my mother, Nawal Abbassi, the exceptional lawyer who taught me the fundamentals of law.
To my wife, Dr. Aml Raafat, a joy in my life.

Contents

Foreword

Give the rich history of common law and legislative attention to the facts necessary to constitute guilt in a criminal case, one would assume that all matters of importance relevant to these foundation issues would have been long settled; that there would be no confusion among prosecutors and defense attorneys about the elements of offenses, the mental states required for those offenses, and the burden of proof as to all relevant issues; and that this information would now be readily communicated clearly and unambiguously to juries who could then apply the facts to clear statements of the law.

Yet, nearly every term of the United States Supreme Court seems to bring another issue of significance to the Court for decision in application of the Winship principle and its many nuances. The most recent flurry of cases, starting with *Apprendi vs. New Jersey*, seems not an ending point but another significant path yet to be fully explored. What is demonstrated is the difficulty and importance of the application of the blameworthiness principle in criminal law systems that are changing rapidly in response to new challenges to our crime control apparatus and to our commitment to basic fairness in criminal cases. Without being able to identify what the next issue will be, I can say with some confidence that there will be new developments in the application of the Winship principle and that they are likely to be related to the mental states required for crimes.

Hisham Ramadan's work therefore comes at a propitious time. Old issues are as yet fully explored; new challenges lie before us. That many of the issues he addresses are not new, yet remain unsettled, and benefit from his careful analysis, signifies the difficulty of clear expression of the mental states required for crimes and the great challenge in expressing those mental states in language that allows the requirements to be applied daily.

It is axiomatic that the very legitimacy of the criminal law depends upon clarity of expression of the facts necessary to constitute guilt in criminal cases in general and in the mental state signifying blameworthiness in particular. This work is a significant step in fortifying this important foundation of criminal law.

Walter J. Dickey
Evjue-Bascom Professor
University of Wisconsin Law School

Preface

My primary objective in writing this book is to explain the law of homicide to the jury in plain and simple language. The first step in my project was to find a very basic statutory and judicial common ground on which I could establish and propose comprehensible jury instructions. Although I was aware of various theoretical backgrounds, laws, and statutory interpretations, I was unaware of the magnitude of the controversy. Generally there was inconsistency in the laws and judicial interpretation at every level in every state. The problem was not a lack of good drafting of jury instructions but rather a lack of a coherent theoretical framework, as well as a lack of consistent laws and uniform statutory interpretation that is essential to the drafting of jury instructions. In some cases, as in negligence, I found several theoretical foundations, but on closer examination they were revealed to be erroneous and inapplicable. Accordingly, I had to tackle the problem at its roots. In this book I discuss the law of homicide to illustrate the historical background and to correct a misunderstanding of very basic concepts. My second step is to expose the underlying rationales and objectives of the law of homicide. These are the components of proper and successful jury instructions. The analysis is doctrinal rather than formalistic. My third step is to create a theoretically sound foundation. In doing so, I attempt to avoid the theoretical and structural problems of the past. Lastly I propose jury instructions based upon the suitable theories and the compelling objectives of the law of homicide.

To ease the reader's tasks, I have deliberately made the discussion as concise as possible without infringing on the ideas and concepts. Although this book has undergone many revisions, it is far from perfect. It may contain mistakes unrecognized at the time of its writing. My hope is to provoke the legal community to discuss the law in a comprehensive form. It is my hope that rather than discussing theories solely or merely addressing a particular issue within the law of homicide, the legal literature will take on a more comprehensive form in order to address the law of homicide from its inception, which is the underlying theories and objectives, to its application, which is jury instruction.

Hisham M. Ramadan
LL.B, LL.M, LL.M (Criminal Law), S.J.D.
Remington Fellow, University of Wisconsin Law School

Acknowledgments

I am deeply indebted to Professor Walter J. Dickey, without whom this book would never have been conceived or written. His input as a mentor has been vital to the development of numerous ideas and concepts presented throughout this publication.

I also owe special thanks to Professors Michael E. Smith and David Schultz for insightful comments on the early drafts and for their support, inspiration, and wisdom.

Chapter One

The Standard of Proof in Criminal Trials: The Challenge of Explaining "Reasonable Doubt"*

I. INTRODUCTION

A very simple doctrine that anchors our justice system is that the party who alleges particular facts bears the burden of proving them. In civil trials, the plaintiff bears the burden of proving the alleged facts that give rise to the claim. Similarly, in criminal trials, the state bears the burden of proving particular facts that constitute the essential elements of the offense charged. Some burdens of proof used in civil trials can be expressed clearly, such as preponderance of evidence or balance of probabilities. The plaintiff must prove that the facts alleged are more probable than not or that there is "slightly stronger evidence in favor of the proponent than that in favor of the contestant."[1]

The expression of the standards of proof in criminal trials can be problematic. The problem emerges when the judge explains "beyond a reasonable doubt.". The United States Supreme Court insisted in *In Re Winship,*[2] that "beyond a reasonable doubt" is a constitutional requirement. The Court also held that the Constitution neither prohibits the trial courts from defining reasonable doubt nor requires them to do so as a matter of course.[3] This has not

---

* Reprinted from volume 40 issue # 1 of the Criminal Law Bulletin with the permission of Thomson West. Further reproductction of any kind is strictly prohibited.

[1] Barton L. Ingraham, *The Right of Silence, The Presumption of Innocence, The Burden of Proof, and a Modest Proposal: A Reply to O' Reilly*, 86 J. Crim. L. & Criminology 559,573 (1996).

[2] *In Re* Winship, 397 U.S. 358 (1970).

[3] *See* Hopt v. Utah, 120 U.S. 340, 440-441 (1887) *aff'd in* Victor v. Nebraska, 511 U.S. 1, 5 (1994) (holding that the Constitution does not require that any particular words be used

stopped the states from engaging in definition mania in an attempt to explain to the jury the degree of certainty required for conviction.[4]

The United States Supreme Court's position has in effect unconditionally licensed the lower courts to interpret and apply "beyond a reasonable doubt" as they desire.[5] The natural consequence is that trial judges, although restricted to the "beyond a reasonable doubt" formula, are liberated from its highest degree of evidential certainty if they explain it in a manner that significantly lowers the state's burden of proof.

This chapter first examines the "beyond a reasonable doubt" standard. It concludes that the standard is not self-explanatory and, if left undefined, creates grave risk of erroneous verdicts. The chapter then examines various ways the "beyond a reasonable doubt" standard has been expressed and argues they are unsatisfactory. It recommends that we go back to first principles, decide what values we mean to convey with the phrase, and rework our explanation of the standard accordingly. After an analysis of the history of the phrase the chapter considers to which facts it is meant to apply. Relying on history and the views of the Canadian Supreme Court, the chapter argues for an expansive view of what must be proved beyond a reasonable doubt, a view at odds with current law in the United States. It concludes with proposed explanations of the phrase, applying them as current law would, and adopting the Canadian view of the facts necessary to constitute guilt.

---

in instructing the jury of the government's burden of proof). *See also* Taylor v. Kentucky, 436 U.S. 478, 485-486 (1978).

[4] *See, e.g.*, California jury instructions define reasonable doubt as, "it is not mere possible doubt, because everything relating to human affairs is open to some possible or imaginary doubt. It is that State of the case which, after entire comparison and consideration of all evidence, leaves the minds of the jurors in that condition that they cannot say they feel an abiding conviction of the truth of the charge." CALIFORNIA JURY INSTRUCTIONS, CRIMINAL, 6th ed. CALJIC Section 2.90. In Virginia, it is defined as, "reasonable doubt is a doubt based on your sound judgment after a full and impartial consideration of all evidence in the case." VIRGINIA MODEL JURY INSTRUCTIONS, CRIMINAL, Instruction number 2.100 (1998). Massachusetts uses the language of "feel abiding conviction to a moral certainty." MASSACHUSETTS JURY INSTRUCTIONS, CRIMINAL 2d ed., instruction No. 1-2 (2000).

[5] State v. Bryan, 287 So. 2d 73 (Fla. 1973) (Florida Supreme court gives trial judges wide discretion to amend pattern jury instructions according to the judge's *feeling* of the case), United States v. Daniels, 986 F.2d 451, 456-57 (11th Cir. 1993) (recognizing broad discretion of trial judge in formulating instruction); United States v. Nolasco, 926 F. 2d 869, 872 (9th Cir. 1991) (placing authority to define reasonable doubt within sound discretion of trial court).

II. IS "BEYOND A REASONABLE DOUBT" A SELF-EXPLANATORY CONCEPT?

Some judges have assumed that all people who are potential jurors should understand this phrase equally and with ease.[6] Empirical research undermines the view that "beyond a reasonable doubt" is a self-explanatory concept.

In an empirical study, psychologists proffered various definitions of "beyond a reasonable doubt" to groups of mock jurors.[7] The verdict of the mock jurors was totally dependant on the instructions. Those who were instructed that any doubt about the defendant's guilt would suffice as a reasonable doubt were much more willing to acquit than those who were told that the doubt must be substantial.[8] Furthermore, the impact of the various definitions of "beyond a reasonable doubt" on various mock juror groups did not affect their perception of the weight of the evidence against the defendant.[9] Largely, this study suggests that the concept of reasonable doubt was not obvious to the mock jurors when it was left undefined.[10]

One study illustrates the comprehension gap between judges and jurors regarding the degrees of certainty required for conviction. A group of judges and jurors were asked to quantify "preponderance of evidence" and "beyond a reasonable doubt" as a percentage of certainty required to enter a judgment. Both groups reported a higher percentage for the "beyond a reasonable doubt" standard than for the "preponderance of evidence" standard.[11] However, the jurors put the "beyond a reasonable doubt" percentage closer to the "preponderance" percentage than did the judges.[12]

One of the problems with the criminal standard of proof arises from the word *reasonable,* which is a qualifying adjective, referring to the degree of

---

[6] *See* United States v. Taylor, 997 F. 2d 1551 (D.C Cir.1993) (holding that "the terms 'reasonable' and 'doubt' are as accessible to laymen as they are to experts. Ordinarily, a district judge may be best advised to attempt no definition of reasonable doubt unless the jury requests it. The purposes of having juries may be best served if juries, in the first instance, bear the responsibility for defining reasonable doubt. Experience has shown that attempts to define reasonable doubt add little in the way of clarity and often add much in the way of confusion and controversy.") *Id.* at 1558. Similar argument was made in Holland v. United States, 348 U.S. 121, 140 (1954).

[7] Norbert. L. Kerr et al., *Guilty Beyond a Reasonable Doubt: Effects of Concept Definition and Assigned Decision Rule on Judgment of Mock Jurors*, 34 J. Personality & Social Psychol 282 (1976).

[8] *Id.* at 291.

[9] *Id.* at 291.

[10] *Id.* at 292.

[11] Rita James Simon & Linda Mahan, *Quantifying Burdens of Proof*, 5 Law & Soc'y Rev. 319 (1971). Very similar results demonstrated in another study conducted in England. *See also* London School of Economics Jury Project, Juries and the Rules of Evidence, 1973 Crim. L. Rev. 208.

[12] *Id.*

certainty required for criminal conviction. This qualifying adjective is subject to interpretation.[13] A survey of United States district judges in the Eastern District of New York indicates that they quantified the degree of certainty in "beyond a reasonable doubt" as low as 76 percent and as high as 95 percent.[14] This wide variance in understanding of the degree of certainty required for conviction permits a variety of standards of proof in criminal trials.

This problem was not produced in a vacuum. It began with the United States Supreme Court's analysis of "beyond a reasonable doubt" in *Victor v. Nebraska.*[15] In that case, the Supreme Court explored a variety of definitions of reasonable doubt. In determining whether jury instructions properly conveyed the notion of "beyond a reasonable doubt," the Court looked at whether the language impressed the fact finder with the need to reach a subjective state of near certitude of guilt of the accused.[16] Such a subjective state promotes various degrees of objective certainty of guilt. In other words, the subjective state of near certitude varies in the mind of each juror. This test is therefore flawed because it is impossible to determine the subjective state of mind of the jurors. The majority opinion in *Victor* asserts that the question is not whether there is a constitutional violation but whether such a violation reasonably affects the decision.[17] Indisputably, the Court's cardinal task is to reveal any constitutional violation and to state the proper rule of law; nevertheless, the majority in *Victor* preferred to speculate as to what the jury might have thought based on the defective instructions. To be sure, this contention is inconsistent with *Winship,* which held that no one knows what the jury might think based on defective instructions, and the risk of confusion in such cases can be so great as to be a violation of the requirement of *Winship.*[18]

---

[13]Irwin A. Horowitz, *Reasonable Doubt Instructions: Commonsense Justice and the Standard of Proof.* 3 Psychol. Pub. Pol'y. & L. 285, 298-299 (1997)(Professor Horowitz after reviewing numerous psychological empirical researches suggests that diverse definitions of "beyond a reasonable doubt" permit the jury to apply a subjective conviction standard that is much lower than the standard understood by lawyers.) He concluded that:

> Because the courts have apparently resisted providing a quantities definition of the reasonable doubt standard and have suggested that it is an inherently qualitative notion, the way seems clear for courts, legislators and citizens to decide that lower certainty of guilt levels are acceptable.

Id. at 300-301.

[14] *See* United States v. Fatico, 458 F. Supp. 388, 410 (S. D. N. Y 1978).

[15] Victor v. Nebraska, 511 U.S. 1 (1994).

[16] *Id.,* at 15 (Quoting Jackson v. Virginia, 443 U.S. 307, 315 (1979)).

[17] *Id.*

[18] Winship, 397 U.S. 358 (1970).

The former abovementioned empirical studies,[19] which are representative of a large body of psychological research, reach the same conclusion: that the phrase "beyond a reasonable doubt" is not self-explanatory. They also suggest that not defining the standard of proof in a criminal trial leaves the juror no choice but to use a standard of proof based on his own "common sense."[20]

The outcome is highly undesirable. The degree of certainty required for conviction varies in the mind of every juror; consequently it is fair to say that many criminals may have escaped punishment when jurors thought that the degree of certainty required for conviction was higher than the one required by law. In addition, a large number of unwarranted convictions may have occurred when jurors thought that the degree of certainty required for conviction was lower than that understood by jurists. Although the United States Supreme Court explicitly placed the risk of jury confusion on the state,[21] many innocent defendants may have been erroneously convicted because of the lack of a comprehensible definition of "beyond a reasonable doubt."

Why did the Supreme Court not define reasonable doubt? A recent article suggests two possible explanations, neither of them entirely satisfactory.[22] The first is that the Supreme Court in *Sandoval v. California*[23] stated that it was unable to define reasonable doubt because of its lack of supervisory power and that any potential interpretation would be inconsistent with the concept of federalism.[24] However, the Court in the earlier case of *Cage v. Louisiana*[25] refused to allow misguided instruction, despite its lack of supervisory power.

These decisions suggest that the lack of supervisory power rationale is a false rationale. It promotes the reversal of state court decisions but leaves state courts without guidance. The second possible explanation is that the Supreme Court thought that reversing *Victor*[26] and insisting on correct instruction might result in numerous retrials and releases of defendants. Such an explanation is weak in view of *Winship*[27] and the Court's assertion at that time that the standard of persuasion "beyond a reasonable doubt" is so fundamental in

---

[19] Kerr et. al., *Supra* note 7, at 292; Simon & Mahan *Supra* note 11; Note, Supra note 13, at 298-299; *see also Supra* text accompanying note 14.

[20] Professor Finkel recognizes that jurors bring a "commonsense" justice into the courtroom. See NORMAN J. FINKEL, COMMONSENSE JUSTICE: JUROR'S NOTIONS OF THE LAW (1995).

[21] *See* Speiser v. Randall, 357 U.S. 513, 525-526 (1958). *See also* Winship, 397 U.S. 369-372 (1970).

[22] Shelagh Kenney, Supreme Court Review: *Fifth Amendment-Upholding the Constitutional Merit of Misleading Reasonable Doubt, Victor v. Nebraska and Sandoval v. California*, 114 S. Ct. 1239 (1994), 85 J. Crim. L. & Criminology 989, 1021-1023 (1995).

[23] Sandoval v. California, 511 U.S. 1 (1994).

[24] *Id.* at 17.

[25] Cage v. Louisiana, 498 U.S. 39 (1990).

[26] Victor v. Nebraska, 511 U.S. 1 (1994).

[27] Winship, 397 U.S. 358 (1970).

criminal law that failure to apply this standard will bring great injustice and will lead ordinary citizens to mistrust the criminal justice system.

The Supreme Court is the ultimate authority on interpreting the United States Constitution. Therefore, the United States Supreme Court bears the inescapable task of interpreting "beyond a reasonable doubt." The argument of the lack of supervisory power confuses the sharp distinction between state law, which may not be subject to United States Supreme Court review, and the court's fundamental task of interpreting the constitutional requirements of the "beyond a reasonable doubt" standard.

III. THE IMPACT OF AN UNDEFINED STANDARD OF PROOF IN CRIMINAL TRIALS

Requiring "beyond a reasonable doubt"[28] and at the same time refraining from a proper explanation[29] results in profound disagreement between courts. Two federal circuit courts have prohibited trial courts from defining "beyond a reasonable doubt."[30] A number of circuit courts of appeals have left the issue of

---

[28]*In Re* Winship, 397 U.S.358 (1970). Failure to instruct a jury on the necessity of proof of guilt beyond a reasonable doubt can never be harmless error. See Cool v. United States, 409 U.S. 100 (1972); Taylor v. Kentucky, 436 U.S. 478 (1978). I doubt that the "beyond a reasonable doubt" formula was ever required or intended by the framers of the Constitution. The dissenters in Winship rightly concluded that the Due Process of Law Clause never expressly or implicitly required the beyond a reasonable doubt standard. They asserted that Due Process of Law does not mean anything more than the law of the land. The drafters of the United States Constitution did not invent the notion of Due Process of Law. It is an old concept rooted in English law since the fourteenth century. A statute passed during the reign of King Edward the Third reads:

> [W]hereas it is contained in the great charter of the franchises of England, that none shall be imprisoned nor put out of his freehold, nor out of his franchises nor free custom, unless it be by the law of the land; it is accorded, assented, and established, that from henceforth none shall be taken by petition or suggestion made to our Lord the king, or to his council, unless it be by indictment or presentment of the good and lawful people of the same neighborhood where such deeds be done, in due manner, or by process made by writ original at the common law; nor that none be ousted of his franchise, nor of his freeholds, unless he be duly brought into question; and forejudged of the same by the course of the law; and if any thing be done against the same, it shall be redressed and holden for none.
>
> 25 Edw. III (A.D. 1351), Stat. 5, c.4.

[29] *See* Victor v. Nebraska, 511 U.S. 1 (1994). The Constitution does not require that any particular form of words be used in advising the jury of the government's burden of proof. *See* Taylor v. Kentucky, 436 U.S. 478, 485-486 (1978).

[30] *See* United States v. Glass, 846 F. 2d 386, 387 (7th Cir. 1988). *See also* United States v. Hall, 854 F. 2d 1036, 1039 (7th Cir. 1988) (The court stated that the definition of reasonable doubt presents a risk without any benefit. The court described attempts to define reasonable doubt as torture and stated that such definitions are "unhelpful to a

defining "beyond a reasonable doubt" to trial judges, who are to formulate in their own language any necessary instructions to the jury.[31] Some other circuits insist that the trial judge must define "reasonable doubt" only if requested.[32]

The Federal Judicial Center's model instruction abandoned the "beyond a reasonable doubt" formula altogether in proposing a new standard directing the jury that they must be "firmly convinced" of guilt before conviction.[33] The courts sent mixed messages in response to this standard. Some approved it,[34] while others, unfortunately, thought it to be an "unnecessary concept."[35] Moreover, some courts adopted a number of problematic definitions of "beyond a reasonable doubt" in an attempt to fill the definitional gap left by the United States Supreme Court. In the following pages I will highlight the most significant definitions.

---

jury" while "at worst, they have the potential to impair a defendant's constitutional right to have the government prove each element beyond a reasonable doubt"). *See also* Hopt v. Utah 120 U.S. 430 (1887)(the United States Supreme Court reached the same conclusion). *See also* United States v. Walton, 207 F. 3d 694, 699 (4th Cir. 2000)(upholding the trial court's refusal to define the standard of proof). Robert C. Power, *Reasonable Doubt and Other Doubts: the Problem of Jury Instructions*. 67 Tenn. L. Rev .45, 119 (1999)(Professor Power criticized these decisions, contending that saying nothing regarding the standard of proof is not a principled approach to improving jury understanding; rather, it is a form of safe harbor in which jury verdicts are upheld as long as a sufficient number of accurate statements are included among the reasonable doubt instructions.)

[31] *See* United States v. Nolasco, 926 F. 2d 869, 872 (9th Cir. 1991) (allocating decision to define reasonable doubt to sound discretion of trial court); United States v. Littlefield, 840 F. 2d 143, 147 (1st Cir. 1988) (asserting that "we do not wish to be interpreted as prescribing a preferred approach"); United States v. Daniels, 986 F.2d 451, 456-57 (11th Cir. 1993) (recognizing broad discretion of trial judge in formulating instruction).

[32] *See* United States v. Hernandez, 176 F. 3d 719, 728 (3d Cir. 1999) (emphasizing that reasonable doubt is not an easy concept for jurors to grasp); Friedman v. United States. 381 F. 2d 155, 160 (8th Cir. 1967) (In the first place it was the court's duty to instruct on the meaning of reasonable doubt and failure to do so upon request would constitute error); Blatt v. United States, 60 F. 2d 481 (3d Cir. 1932) (holding that failure to define constitutes reversible error); United States v. Pepe, 501 F. 2d 1142 (10th Cir. 1974) (establishing defendant's right to have meaning of reasonable doubt explained to jury); United States v. Taylor, 997 F. 2d 1551, 1557 (D.C. Cir. 1993) (recognizing that giving definition remains practice in District of Columbia circuit.).

[33] FEDERAL JUDICIAL Ctr., PATTERN CRIMINAL JURY INSTRUCTIONS No. 21, at 28 (1988).

[34] State v. Medina, 685 A. 2d 1242, 1251-1252 (1996); United States v. Hunt, 794 F. 2d 1095, 1100-1101 (5th Cir. 1986); United States v. Velasquez, 980 F. 2d 1275, 1278-1279 (9th Cir. 1992) (finding that the phrase "firmly convinced" does not understate the burden); United States v. Pungitore, 910 F.2d 1084 (3d Cir. 1990) (endorsing the standard). *See also* Victor v. Nebraska, 511 U.S. 1, 27 (1994) Ginsburg, J. in her concurring opinion in Victor suggested that "firmly convinced" standard for conviction, repeated for emphasis, is further enhanced by the juxtaposed prescription that the jury must acquit if there is "real possibility" that the defendant is innocent).

[35] United States v. Porter, 821 F. 2d 968, 973(4th Cir. 1987).

A. "TO A MORAL CERTAINTY" APPROACH

Some courts favored the old definition of "beyond a reasonable doubt" found in the instruction of Chief Justice Show in *Commonwealth v. Webster.*[36] This instruction emphasizes the presumption of innocence and the high degree of certainty required for conviction.[37] It instructs the jury that they must be convinced "to a moral certainty" before they convict. The United States Supreme Court in *Cage v. Louisiana*[38] rejected instructions containing the phrase "moral certainty" when it was mentioned in conjunction with phrases describing reasonable doubt as something that "would give rise to a grave uncertainty" and "is actual substantial doubt."[39] In rejecting the Louisiana Supreme Court's argument, the Court stated that the use of these phrases might overstate the requisite degree of uncertainty and confuse the jury, but that by "taking the charge as whole" reasonable persons of ordinary intelligence would understand the definition of "beyond a reasonable doubt."[40] The Court held that "it is plain to us the words 'substantial' and 'grave,' as they are commonly understood, suggest a higher degree of doubt than is required for acquittal under the reasonable doubt standard."[41] "When those statements are then considered in reference to moral certainty rather than evidentiary certainty, it becomes clear that a reasonable juror could have interpreted the instructions to allow a finding of guilt below that required by the Due Process Clause."[42]

Cage was followed by *Sullivan v. Louisiana,*[43] in which the trial judge gave a definition of "reasonable doubt" that was essentially identical to the one held unconstitutional in *Cage.*[44] The Court reaffirmed *Cage's* judgment, adding that *Sullivan's* instruction denies the right to trial by jury.[45]

In *Victor,*[46] the Court was again confronted with an instruction very similar to those in *Cage* and *Sullivan*. However, the Court upheld the instructions, holding that "the proper inquiry is not whether the instruction 'could have' been applied in an unconstitutional manner, but whether there is reasonable likelihood that the jury did so apply it."[47] The Court admitted that the

---

[36] Commonwealth v. Webster, 5 Cush. 295 (1850).
[37] *See* Commonwealth v. Pinckney, 419 Mass. 341,345 (1995)(Failure to stress the degree of certainty required for conviction, in conjunction with the phrase "moral certainty," requires reversal.)
[38] Cage v. Louisiana, 498 U.S. 39 (1990).
[39] *Id.* at 41.
[40] *Id.* at 40-41.
[41] *Id.* at 41.
[42] *Id.* at 41.
[43] Sullivan v. Louisiana, 508 U.S. 275 (1993).
[44] *Id.* at 277.
[45] *Id.*
[46] Victor v. Nebraska, 511 U.S. 1 (1994).
[47] *See* Estelle v. McGuire, 502 U.S. 62, 72 (1991).

phrase "moral certainty" is ambiguous.[48] Nevertheless, it is acceptable when read in context. The "read in context" argument that was rejected in *Cage* became the anchor in *Victor*.

Victor's hesitant decision encourages the lower courts to ignore the United States Supreme Court's hostility to the "moral certainty" approach. Although the Court considered it an ambiguous and disfavored explanation of the standard of proof, "moral certainty" was endorsed by both lower courts and legislatures. It was mentioned fifteen times in one approved instruction.[49] Astonishingly, most circuits upheld this disfavored phrase.[50] Massachusetts's pattern jury instructions acknowledge the United States Supreme Court's hostility to the "moral certainty" phrase but nevertheless recommended it.[51]

Professor Barbara Shapiro explored the origin of the phrase "moral certainty." She concluded that historically the highest level of certainty, although no absolute certainty is possible, is what traditionally has been called "moral certainty."[52] However, what has been linguistically proper in the past does not necessarily reflect our understanding of an archaic concept.[53]

The deficiency in the definition of "moral certainty" exceeds the mere fact that it is archaic. It is a vague concept, subject to interpretation. Professor Horowitz, a psychology professor, concluded that jurors might construe the phrase "moral certainty" to mean that one may give weight to one's personal and moral standards, especially if the trial involves moral issues.[54] Therefore, when the law seems unfair or the defendant inspires sympathy, a jury may be reluctant to convict.[55] On the other hand, when the crime is heinous, the jury may be more likely to be punitive.[56] In essence, "moral certainty" instructions offer an indirect invitation to nullify the law.[57]

The weight of Professor Horowitz's argument becomes clear in cases where morality is appealing to jurors. In *Buckoke v. Greater London Council*,[58]

---

[48] Victor v. Nebraska, 511 U.S. 1, 14 (1994).
[49] Williams v. Matesanz, 230 F. 3d 421 (1st Cir. 2000).
[50] Austin v. Bell, 126 F. 3d 843, 846-867 (6th Cir. 1997); Dupuy v. Cain, 201 F. 3d 582, 587 (5th Cir. 2000); Gilday v. Callahan, 59 F. 3d 257, 262 (1st Cir. 1995); Felker v. Trupin, 83 F. 3d 1303, 1310 (11th Cir. 1996); United States v. Jacobs, 44 F. 3d 1219, 1225 (3d Cir. 1995).
[51] MASSACHUSETTS JURY INSTRUCTIONS, CRIMINAL 2d ed., Instruction No. 1-2 (2000).
[52] Barbara J. Shapiro, *"To a Moral Certainty": Theories of Knowledge and Anglo-American Juries 1600-1850*, 38 Hastings L. J. 153, 192-193 (1986).
[53] Sandoval v. California, 511 U.S. 1 (1994). *See also* the concurrence of Kennedy, J. *Id.* at 23(stating "what once might have made sense to jurors has long since becomes archaic).
[54] Irwin A. Horowitz, *Reasonable Doubt Instructions: Commonsense Justice and the Standard of Proof.* 3 Psychol. Pub. Pol'y. & L. 285, 288 (1997).
[55] *Id.*
[56] *Id.* at 288-289.
[57] *Id.* at 288-289.
[58] Buckoke v. Greater London Council [1971] 2 ALL E. R. 254.

Lord Denning explained the following hypothetical: a driver of a fire engine with ladders approaches the traffic light.[59] He sees a blazing house two hundred yards down the road, with a man at the upstairs window in extreme peril.[60] The traffic light is red; if the defendant waited for the traffic light to turn green, the man in peril would die.[61] The defendant ran the red light and saved the man in peril.[62] If the defendant argues necessity defense his plea should be denied.[63]

Lord Denning recognized the moral dimension, contending, "Nevertheless such a man should not be prosecuted. He should be congratulated."[64] In this case, a well-trained judge could not refrain from commenting on the moral dimension of the case. However, Lord Denning believed that the hypothetical defendant should be convicted because traffic laws are designed to protect innocent drivers. A layperson instructed to apply the moral certainty standard is likely to acquit, which would frustrate the purpose of traffic laws.

By using "moral certainty," we are asking jurors to shift their minds from a fact-finding function in following the legal rules to the moral question of whether the defendant *should* be convicted. In sum, applying the moral certainty standard does not resolve the problem; rather we exchange one problematic standard for another that is even more problematic.[65]

B. THE ANALOGY APPROACH

One of the popular definitions of "beyond a reasonable doubt" is commonly called the analogy approach. It commands the jurors to draw an analogy between the certainty required to make a decision in their lives and the certainty required for conviction. The analogy approach takes a number of forms, one of which formulates the concept in general terms to require the jury to make a decision as they would make decisions in their own lives.[66] Another detailed formula for the analogy approach directs the jury to the type of doubt that would cause them to *hesitate to act* in an important decision in their lives.[67]

---

[59] *Id.* at 258
[60] *Id.* at 258
[61] *Id.* at 258
[62] *Id.* at 258
[63] *Id.* at 258
[64] *Id.* at 258
[65] *See* Commonwealth v. Kloiber, 378 Pa.412, 106 A.2d 820 (1954)(The Supreme Court of Pennsylvania held that the use of the phrase "moral certainty" merely "serves to confuse the jury instead of enlightening them").
[66] *See* United States v. Holland, 348 U.S. 121 (1954); Hopt v. Utah, 120 U.S. 430 (1887).
[67] Wills v. State, 329 MD. 370 (1993). *See also* United States v. De Lazo, 497 F. 2d1168, 1171 (3d Cir. 1974), United States v. Velasquez, 980 F. 2d 1275 (9th Cir. 1992); Taylor v. Kentucky, 436 U.S. 478 (1978)(The courts concluded that the phrase "firmly convinced" is similar to "hesitate to act.").

In *Wills v. State*,[68] the Maryland Supreme Court correctly concluded that the language "hesitate to act" may mislead the jury.[69] The court reasoned that the jury may erroneously conclude that reasonable doubt exists because they hesitate to act in arriving at a conviction decision.[70] Interestingly enough, the court suggested the alternative language of "without reservation," found in the Maryland pattern jury instructions.[71] It is not clear why the court did not see the similarity between the "hesitate to act" formula and "without reservation." Both of them concern the immediacy of taking an action. A juror who has an imaginary reservation or fanciful doubt will hesitate to act or convict. Even if the similarity in the language is not obvious, it would be proper to explain to the jury what sort of reservation they can rely on in their decision making. It is important for jurors to know that not every possible reservation, possible doubt, or imaginary doubt suffices to support an acquittal.

The analogy approach, whether formulated in general terms or in specific language, does not provide a satisfactory definition of "beyond a reasonable doubt." A juror might make a decision in his or her life based upon a degree of certainty that is much less than that required by law. A typical juror—as a layperson—might make a life decision after weighing the benefits and losses that may occur from making such a decision. If making a certain decision is likely to generate benefits even slightly outweighing the losses, the juror is likely to make that decision. In other words, a layperson is likely to decide based on "more probable than not." This standard of decision making is characterized in law as preponderance of the evidence. If the decision involves an important matter, the layperson is likely to require a clear indication that he is making the right choice; this standard of decision making is closely related to the legal standard of clear and convincing evidence. Only in some situations does the layperson visualize the highest degree of certainty required in the "beyond a reasonable doubt" standard. Largely, the analogy approach fails because it directs jurors to a flawed standard of proof, ranging from the highest degree of certainty to the lowest.

C. "BEYOND A SUBSTANTIAL DOUBT" APPROACH

Although the Supreme Court acknowledges in *Victor v. Nebraska*[72] that defining the source of the doubt as "substantial doubt" is somewhat problematic,[73] it concluded that "substantial doubt" is to be accepted because of

---

[68] Wills v. State, 329 MD. 370 (1993).
[69] *Id.* at 383.
[70] *Id.* at 384.
[71] *Id.* at 384.
[72] Victor v. Nebraska, 511 U.S 1 (1994).
[73] *Id.* at 19.

its context within the instructions.[74] Justice O'Connor considered "substantial" to refer to a doubt's existence rather than to its quantum.[75]

The phrases "grave doubt" and "substantial doubt" overstate the degree of doubt required to acquit.[76] Consequently, the degree of certainty of guilt is lowered far below what was required in *Winship*. If the Supreme Court justices did not find that the word "substantial" significantly increases the quantum of doubt required for acquittal, thus, in effect, decreasing the degree of certainty required for conviction, then the premise of this chapter has an uphill fight to gain acceptance.

To be sure, *Victor's* jury instruction did not contain any statement correcting the error of the "substantial doubt" phrase. But the Supreme Court may have chosen to "wrap up" an unsatisfactory instruction under the test of "reading in context"[77] or "totality of the circumstances"[78] to avoid later overruling or modification. Assuming that the Supreme Court argument bears some validity, it is nevertheless unfortunate that the nation's highest court refrained from providing lower courts with some guidelines to deal with the standard of proof in criminal trials, a matter of the utmost importance.

Interestingly enough, the test of "totality of the circumstances" or "reading the whole instruction in context" is an elastic concept. The Court justices stretch this test in some cases and disregard it in others. In *Sandstrom v. Montana,*[79] Justice Brennan delivered a unanimous decision acknowledging that when there are two possible interpretations of the state court's instruction, one could not be certain on which interpretation the jury based its decision. Such uncertainty renders the instructions unconstitutional, requiring reversal. Applying this principle to *Victor*, there were at least two possible interpretations of "beyond a reasonable doubt." One is that the burden of proof was properly stated. The other is that the state overstated the degree of doubt required for acquittal by directing the jury that the doubt must be substantial, which consequently understated the state's burden of proof. In light of *Sandstrom*, *Victor* ought to be overruled because we will never know for certain the basis of

---

[74] *Id.* at 20.
[75] *Id.* at 20.
[76] The phrases "grave doubt" and "substantial doubt" must be distinguished from "real doubt," a phrase that seems to be widely accepted because it shows that imaginary doubt is not sufficient to acquit. Many courts accepted the definition of "real doubt." *See* United States v. Conway, 73 F. 3d 975, 980 (10th Cir. 1995). (The court rejects the contention that the use of "real doubt" impermissibly shifts the burden of proof.) *See also* United States v. Hunt, 794 F. 2d 1095 (5th Cir. 1986)(The Fifth Circuit characterizes the challenge to the "real possibility" as ridiculous.)
[77] *See* Holland v. United States, 348 U.S. 121, 140 (1954)(The United States Supreme Court held that a problematic jury instruction, "taken as a whole… [must] correctly convey the concept of reasonable doubt to the jury."). This test was confirmed in Victor v. Nebraska, 511 U.S. 1 (1994).
[78] Kentucky v. Whorton, 441 U.S. 86 (1979).
[79] Sandstrom v. Montana, 442 U.S. 510 (1979).

the jury's decision; but the magical test of "reading in context" saved the case from destined reversal.[80]

IV. THE BASIC CONCEPTS IN "BEYOND A REASONABLE DOUBT" INSTRUCTIONS

Although the United States Supreme Court decisively commanded the use of "beyond a reasonable doubt" instructions,[81] the Constitution does not literally use the phrase "beyond a reasonable doubt."[82] It is merely a phrase containing two important concepts firmly rooted in the justice system. These concepts are the presumption of innocence and the degree of proof required for conviction, or the quantum of proof.[83] Although the presumption of innocence is not explicitly stated in the "beyond a reasonable doubt" phrase, it is implied by the notion that until all reasonable doubt has been removed, the defendant is presumed innocent. Therefore, I will explore the origins of these concepts and suggest what their application might be in our justice system.

A. HISTORICAL BACKGROUND

The earliest form of jury instruction is found in the thirteen century in Bracton's writing. The instruction was phrased in terms of faith in God and the principals of Christianity.[84] It directs the jury to two essential concepts, namely, lack of bias and the degree of certainty required for conviction.[85] Jurors were required to

---

[80] *See* Sandstrom v. Montana, 442 U.S. 510,526 (1979)(Justice Brennan's analysis of Sandstrom based upon the rejection of "jury speculation" as to the meaning of the instructions. If we did not know for certain the basis for the verdict, we should reverse the case. It was suggested, "Even if a jury could have ignored the presumption and found defendant guilty because he acted knowingly, we cannot be certain that this is what they *did* do .As the jury verdict was a general one, we have no way of knowing that Sandstrom was not convicted on the basis of the unconstitutional instruction."). *See Id.*

[81] *See* Cool v. United States, 409 U.S. 100 (1972); Taylor v. Kentucky, 436 U.S. 478 (1978)(Failure to instruct a jury on the necessity of proof of guilt beyond a reasonable doubt can never be harmless error).

[82] *See* Winship, 397 U.S. 358, 377 (It was stated "the court has never clearly held, however, that proof beyond a reasonable doubt is either expressly or impliedly commanded by the Constitution.") (Chief Justice Burger and Justice Stewart dissenting).

[83] GLANVILLE WILLIAMS, TEXTBOOK OF CRIMINAL LAW, 108 (1978)(According to Williams, the phrase "'beyond a reasonable doubt' is virtually indefinable…A judge in summing up should convey two separate points to the jury: that the burden of proof is on the prosecution, and that they must feel sure of guilt (or words to that effect)").

[84] 2 BRACTON, ON THE LAWS AND CUSTOMS OF ENGLAND, PLEAS OF THE CROWN 405 (Samuel E. Thorne ed., Harvard University Press 1968).

[85] The actual text says, "And therefore we tell you that on the faith that bind you to God and by the oath that you have taken you are to let us know the truth thereof, nor are you

be confident of guilt as "with God only before your eyes."[86] Hence, the degree of certainty required for conviction was left to the *satisfied conscience* of the jurors. The test of "satisfied conscience" continues to appear in many cases throughout the seventeenth century.[87] It merely commands the jury to be satisfied of guilt, without any reference to the degree of certainty required for conviction.

Gradually, the notion of proving the offense "beyond a reasonable doubt" began to crystallize. Sir Mathew Hale pointed out that in *reasonable circumstances* the jury needs only *just cause* to suspect the credibility of the evidence.[88] The phrase "just cause" was the synonym of the modern phrase "reasonable doubt" in the sense that the jurors need only just cause—or reasonable doubt—to acquit.

In the eighteenth century the phrase "beyond a reasonable doubt" was clearly adopted in the famous Boston Massacre trials of 1770[89] and in the Irish treason trials of 1798.[90] However, it is very difficult to pinpoint the first case that adopted the "beyond a reasonable doubt" phrase and therefore to understand the historical penal policy underlying it.[91] Until the nineteenth century, the common law is generally silent on how or why the phrase "beyond a reasonable

---

to fail in saying whether or not he is guilty of what is alleged against him (or of the other crimes) through fear or love or hate but with God only before your eyes, nor are you to oppress him if he be innocent of the said offense." See *Id.*

86 *Id.*

87 *See* Green's Case, 7 How. St. Tr. 159, 220 (1679), Moder's Case, 6 How. St. Tr. 274, 282 (1663). The language, "satisfied of guilt," continued to appear in the eighteenth century. *See also* Regina v. Brady, 168 Eng. Rep. 267 (1784).

88 MATTHEW HALE, THE HISTORY OF THE COMMON LAW OF ENGLAND, 346 (6th ed., Henry Butterworth, law-bookseller 1820) Hale states:

> And indeed, it is one of the excellencies of the trial, above the trial by witness, that although the jury ought to give great regard to witnesses and their testimony, YET THEY ARE NOT ALWAYS BOUND BY IT; but may either upon reasonable circumstances, inducing a blemish upon their creditability, though otherwise in themselves in strictness of law they are to be heard, pronounce a verdict CONTRARY to such testimonies; the truth whereof they have just cause to suspect, and may DO OFTEN, pronounce their verdict upon one single testimony; which the civil law admits not of.

Id.

89 *See* 3 L. WORTH & H. ZOBEL, LEGAL PAPERS OF JOHN ADAMS (1965). For further analysis *see* Anthony A. Morano, *A Reexamination of the Reasonable Doubt Rule*, 55 B.U.L Rev. 507, 516-519 (1975).

90 Finney's Case, 26 How. St. Tr. 1019 (Ir. 1798), Bond's Case, 27 How. St. Tr. 523 (Ir. 1798).

91 Barbara J. Shapiro, *" To a Moral Certainty": Theories of Knowledge and Anglo-American Juries 1600-1850*, 38 Hastings L. J. 153, 171 (1986) (Professor Shapiro believes that the Boston Massacre cases did not suggest that the "beyond a reasonable doubt" standard was considered innovative, for both prosecution and bench emphasized that the accused were being tried according to traditional English usage).

doubt" was adopted.[92] Even the presumption of innocence was not taken seriously in this era.[93]

It appears that by the nineteenth century, the phrase "beyond a reasonable doubt" was being used to implement the presumption of innocence.[94] In some cases the courts maximized the value of the presumption of innocence to require the jury to acquit unless they were satisfied of guilt beyond *all* reasonable doubt.[95] In the recent *Winship* decision, the United States Supreme Court reaffirmed that the standard of "beyond a reasonable doubt" provides concrete substance for the presumption of innocence.[96]

B. THE MODERN ANALYSIS OF THE PRESUMPTION OF INNOCENCE

Reading through Supreme Court analyses of the presumption of innocence suggests two distinct principles. First, the presumption of innocence need not be stated explicitly, but can be *disguised* in jury instructions. In *Kentucky v.*

---

[92]Barbara J. Shapiro, *"To a Moral Certainty": Theories of Knowledge and Anglo-American Juries 1600-1850,* 38 Hastings L. J. 153,170 (1986) (Professor Shapiro concluded that in the eighteenth century the phrase "moral certainty" was taken to mean proof "beyond a reasonable doubt." I disagree with her thesis because it comes without one single authority or case linking the two distinctive concepts).

[93] MICHAEL FOSTER, CROWN LAW 225 (E. and R. Brooke ed., 1792) (Concluding that "In every charge of murder, the fact of killing being first proved, all the circumstances of the accident, necessity, or infirmity are to be satisfactorily proved by the prisoner, unless they arise out of the evidence produced against him; for the law presumes the fact to have been founded in malice, until the contrary appears").

[94] *See* Magee v. Mark, 11 Ir. R..-C.L. 449 (1861) (Pigot C. B.)(He asserted that "The jury ought to have been told to give the benefit of the doubt to the defendant, because until all doubt shall have been removed, the presumption of innocence stands unrebutted."). Davis v. United States, 160 U.S. 469, 485-486 (1895). The court stated:

> The plea of not guilty is unlike a special plea in a civil action which, admitting the case averred, seeks to establish substantive grounds of defense by a preponderance of evidence. It is not confession and avoidance, for it is a plea that controverts the existence of every fact essential to constitute the crime charged. Upon that plea the accused may stand, shielded by the presumption of his innocence, until it appears that he is guilty; if the jury entertains as reasonable doubt from all the evidence whether he was legally capable of committing the crime.

Id.

[95]Regina v. White, 176 Eng. Rep. 611 (1865)(Holding "In a criminal case the jury in order to convict ought to be satisfied that by the evidence, affirmatively, as a conviction created in their minds beyond all reasonable doubt, the guilt of the prisoner is established, and if there is only an impression of probability, they ought to acquit him.").

[96] Winship, 397 U.S. 358, 363 (1970).

Whorton,[97] the Court held that "the failure to give a requested instruction on the presumption of innocence does not in and of itself violate the constitution."[98] The test of whether the Constitution was violated by failure to give an adequate presumption of innocence instruction is the totality of the circumstances.[99]

The second principle is that the states, including their judicial and legislative branches, should not undermine the presumption of innocence by shifting the burden of proof, all or in part, to the defendant. In a series of cases, the United States Supreme Court correctly reversed cases in which jury instructions improperly shifted the burden of proof by allowing the jury to presume one of the elements of the offense.[100]

In recent decisions, the Court reversed cases in which the presumption of innocence was diminished by lowering the standard of proof from "beyond a reasonable doubt" to a mere "preponderance of the evidence."[101] In this type of case, the legislature unconstitutionally removes from the jury the assessment of facts that increase the prescribed range of penalties to which a criminal defendant is exposed.[102]

Remarkably, in recent cases the United States Supreme Court examined the issue of presumption of innocence only as a requirement of *Winship*. Its analysis falls short of offering a comprehensive scheme to guide state courts and legislatures. The lack of a theoretical framework is likely to cause future erroneous and unconstitutional jury instructions. For instance, in *Apprendi v. New Jersey*,[103] the Supreme Court held that any fact (other than a prior conviction) that increases the penalty for a crime beyond the prescribed statutory maximum must be submitted to a jury, and proved beyond a reasonable doubt.[104] The dissent asserted that this holding permits state legislatures to reallocate the burden of proof by labeling some elements of the offenses as affirmative defenses. The majority held that the right of state legislatures to create affirmative defenses is subject to constitutional limitations.[105] The Court did not

---

[97] Kentucky v. Whorton, 441 U.S. 786 (1979).

[98] *Id.* at 789.

[99] Taylor v. Kentucky, 436 U.S. 478 (1978) (Under *Taylor*, the failure to instruct on the presumption of innocence must be evaluated in light of the totality of the circumstances—including all the instructions to the jury, the arguments of counsel, whether the weight of the evidence was overwhelming, and other factors relevant to determining whether the defendant received a constitutionally fair trial.).

[100] Sandstrom v. Montana, 442 U.S. 510 (1979); Francis v. Franklin, 471 U.S. 307 (1985); Mullaney v, Wilbur, 421 U.S. 684 (1975); Rose v. Clark, 478 U.S. 570 (1986); Connecticut v. Johnson, 460 U.S. 73 (1983). *See also* County Court of Ulster County v. Allen, 442 U.S. 140 (1979)(The U.S. Supreme Court allowed a permissive presumption which the prosecutor can rely on, so long as it does not shift the burden of proof and can be rebutted by contrary evidence.).

[101] Jones v. United States, 526 U.S. 227(1999), *aff'd*, 530 U.S. 466 (2000).

[102] *Id.*

[103] Apprendi v. New Jersey, 530 U.S. 466 (2000).

[104] *Id.* at 490.

[105] *Id.* at 485.

define the extent of the limitations or the scheme to be followed by legislatures to avoid unconstitutionality.

C. PROPOSED ALTERNATIVE INTERPRETATION OF THE PRESUMPTION OF INNOCENCE

1. Contrasting Theories of Innocence: Canadian versus American

The Canadian Supreme Court offers a coherent, comprehensive scheme guiding the lower courts' expression of the presumption of innocence. The Court argues that when the possibility of reasonable doubt exists, the presumption of innocence is breached.[106] The categorization of a factor as an excuse, justification, or essential element of an offense should not affect the presumption of innocence analysis.[107] It is the effect of that factor that is crucial.[108] If the defendant is required to prove or disprove a factor—whether it is "excuse," "defense," or even "essential element"—to avoid conviction, the presumption of innocence is defeated because conviction can occur despite reasonable doubt in the mind of the trier of fact as to guilt.[109] The implied proposition is that the defendant must be shielded by the presumption of innocence during a trial until every fact exonerating the defendant or decreasing the penalty is disproven "beyond a reasonable doubt." Yet, a necessary qualifier for the Canadian approach is that only facts put in issue must be "disproved." There is no need to disprove a self-explanatory fact not placed in issue.

This simple, plausible analysis is much easier to understand than the artificial distinctions so often drawn by the United States Supreme Court. The Court, in *Patterson v. New York*,[110] upheld a New York law allowing the defendant to prove extreme emotional distress as an affirmative defense to murder, while *Mullaney v. Wilbur*[111] invalidated a Maine statute that presumes that a defendant possesses the "malice aforethought" necessary to constitute murder. In both cases, the requirement that the defendant prove *a fact* to avoid conviction undermines the presumption of innocence. In *Apprendi v. New Jersey*,[112] the Court distinguished *Patterson* from *Mullaney* by stating that New York state law still requires the state to prove every element of the offense beyond a reasonable doubt. Why did the Court hold that the state did not have to prove lack of emotional distress as an element of the offense? Does the label of a fact control its nature? Are there any constitutional guidelines demonstrating the proper definition of the elements of the offense? The distinction between

---

106 R. v. Whyte (1988) 51 DLR (4th) 481, 493.
107 *Id.*
108 *Id.*
109 *Id.*
110 Patterson v. New York, 432 U.S. 197 (1977).
111 Mullaney v. Wilbur, 421 U.S. 684 (1975).
112 Apprendi v. New Jersey, 530 U.S. 466, 485 (2000).

Mullaney and *Patterson* would properly stand if we had a table defining the constitutionally proper elements of offenses. So long as this imaginary table does not exist, the Canadian Supreme Court's analysis will be the best clarification of the presumption of innocence.

Winship's narrow interpretation of the presumption of innocence is far from conclusive. In *Ulster County v. Allen*,[113] the Supreme Court stretched the scope of the presumption of innocence by requiring proof of the mandatory presumptions beyond a reasonable doubt.[114] In *Apprendi*,[115] the Supreme Court went beyond *Winship*, which requires submitting to the jury and proving "*every fact necessary to prove the offense.*" *Apprendi* requires submitting to the jury and proving "*any fact that increases the penalty*" beyond the statutory maximum with the exception of recidivism. In each of these challenges the Supreme Court tried to compensate for deficiencies in the application of the presumption of innocence, while the Canadian approach would not have encountered such challenges.

The differences between the Canadian and American approaches are clear. The Canadian approach focuses on the defendant's responsibility, asserting that a defendant cannot be obliged to prove anything without breaching the presumption of innocence. On the other hand, the American approach focuses on the state's duties, emphasizing that the state must prove every fact necessary to prove the offense. The Canadian approach recognizes that the presumption of innocence is designed primarily to protect innocent defendants from erroneous convictions.[116] The American analysis stems from the *Winship* decision, in which the court used the presumption of innocence doctrine to define the state's burden of proof. It would have been more proper for the Supreme Court to adopt the defendant's point of view by asserting that the presumption of innocence is designed to protect the innocent defendant; therefore, the defendant is not required to prove anything, because otherwise the presumption is breached.

2. THE DEFICIENCIES IN THE AMERICAN APPROACH

The Supreme Court in *Patterson v. New York*[117] allows the states to place the burden of proof on the defendant in defenses, so long as the state proves the

---

[113] County Court of Ulster County v. Allen, 442 U. S. 140, 99 S. Ct. 2213 (1979).
[114] *Id.* at 169.
[115] Apprendi v. New Jersey, 530 U.S. 466, 485 (2000).
[116] John M. Tyson, *Presumed Guilty Until Proven Innocent: Using Results of Statistical or Economic Studies as Evidence*, 10 St. Thomas L. Rev. 387, 391 (1998) (Concluding that "The presumption of innocence was developed for the purpose of guarding against the conviction of an innocent person...thus, where the prosecution is unable to muster evidence sufficient to overcome the presumption, there will be an acquittal, even though the defendant be actually guilty.").
[117] Patterson v. New York, 432 U.S. 197(1977).

elements of the offense beyond a reasonable doubt.[118] The Court concluded that it should not construe the Constitution to intrude upon the administration of justice by the states[119] "unless in so doing it offends some principle of justice so rooted in the traditions and conscience of our people as to be ranked as fundamental."[120] Therefore, in the Supreme Court's view, the presumption of innocence and the issue of shifting the burden of proof are limited to the elements of the offenses and not the defenses.[121] This approach is invalid for a number of reasons.

First, the presumption of innocence is included in the Due Process Clause of the Fourteenth Amendment because substantive due process means "fundamental fairness."[122] This "fundamental fairness" requires that we presume that every individual is a law-abiding citizen until proven guilty in a court of law. It also requires an assurance that no innocent defendant is erroneously convicted because he failed to prove his innocence, either by failure to negate the offense or *failure to prove a defense, despite lack of incriminating evidence sufficient to convict under the "beyond a reasonable doubt" standard.*

Second, the differentiation in treatment between the elements of offenses and defenses is unfounded. Allocating a specific issue as an element of the offense or the defense depends on convenience or ease of phrasing.[123] Even if there is a hypothetical distinction between the elements of the offenses and the defenses, such a distinction is not clear. For instance, the drafters of the Model Penal Code recognized the overlap between the elements of defenses and offenses in the mistake defense, which could be established by negating one of the mental elements of the offense.[124] Similarly, subsections 1.13 (9) (C) and (D) include negating justification, excuse, and defenses as elements of an offense.[125]

Third, Professor Williams suggests that we must understand the word "offenses" as an "offense package" that consists of the elements of both the offense and the defense(s). The defendant cannot be convicted unless the elements of the offense are proven and the elements of the defense are lacking. When the legislature places the initial burden of proof on the defendant, and the defendant fails to prove the existence of a defense, the defendant can be convicted without the proof of the "offense package." The defendant can be

---

[118] *Id.* at 210

[119] *Id.* at 201-202.

[120] Speiser v. Randall, 357 U.S. 513, 523 (1958); Leland v. Oregon, 343 U.S. 790, 798 (1952).

[121] *See* Mullaney v. Wilbur, 421 U.S. 684 (1975); Patterson v. New York, 432 U.S. 197 (1977).

[122] Winship, 397 U.S. 358, 369 (1970) (Harlan J. concurring).

[123] John Calvin Jeffries Jr. & Paul B. Stephen III, *Defenses, Presumptions and Burden of Proof in the Criminal Trial*, 88 Yale L.J.1232, 1332 (1979). *See also* David Finley, *The Presumption of Innocence and Guilt: Why Carroll Should Prevail Over Oakes*, 39 C.R. (3d) 115,127 (1984).

[124] MODEL PENAL CODE § 2.04(1) (a) (Proposed Official Draft 1962).

[125] MODEL PENAL CODE § 1.13(9) (c) & (d) (Proposed Official Draft 1962).

convicted notwithstanding evidence supporting the defense and lack of evidence disproving it.[126]

For further clarification of the offense package analysis, consider this hypothesis. Mr. Adams is charged with first-degree murder and he intends to raise the issue of self-defense. To convict him, the state must prove the elements of first-degree murder and disprove self-defense. If the state requires Mr. Adams to prove self-defense and he fails, and thereafter the state proves only the elements of first-degree murder beyond a reasonable doubt, his guilt is not proven under the offense package analysis because there might be a reasonable doubt regarding the existence of self-defense.

To further complicate the issue, self-defense is a justification, and justification is a legal and encouraged conduct.[127] To prove his guilt we must prove illegality by disproving self-defense beyond a reasonable doubt. To require Mr. Adams to prove self-defense by preponderance of the evidence is to create unjustifiably a *prima facie* presumption that self-defense did not exist.[128] Whether proof of guilt arises from elements of the offense[129] or defense is irrelevant.

Fourth, there are no explicit rules in the United States Constitution or in common law that allow placing the burden of proof on the defendant.[130] However, allocating the burden of proof on the defendant is supported by two practical considerations: convenience, and the desirability of excluding fanciful defenses.[131] In attempting to strike a balance between the individual's interests and the state's legitimate interests, the risk of erroneous conviction greatly outweighs the state's interests. Accordingly, the legislature must tend to allocate the burden of proof on the state in defenses and offenses alike.

Fifth, limiting the scope of the presumption of innocence to only the elements of the offense, as expressed in *Patterson*, is based on faulty logic. The court allowed the state to place the burden of persuasion on the defendant with respect to affirmative defenses. The logic was that the state is not constitutionally required to provide affirmative defenses at all. Therefore, if the state chooses to do so, it may take lesser steps of placing the burden of proof on the defendant because "greater power includes the lesser."[132] However, the state has unlimited power to define offenses.[133] Therefore, the state has the power to abolish *mens rea* in an offense by defining the offense as strict liability. Thus,

---

[126] Glanville Williams, *The Logic of "Exceptions,"* 47 Camb.L.J.261, 280 (1988).
[127] Paul Robinson, *Criminal Law Defenses: A Systematic Analysis*, 82 Col. L. Rev. 199, 213-221(1982).
[128] *See* similar analysis in Glanville Williams, *The Logic of "Exceptions,"* 47 Camb.L.J.261, 264 (1988).
[129] *See* Mullaney v. Wilbur, 421 U.S. 684 (1975).
[130] Patrick Healy, *Proof and Policy: No Golden Threads*, 72 Crim.L.Rev.355, 362 (1987).
[131] Glanville Williams, *Offenses and Defenses*, 2 Legal Stud. 233, 235 (1982).
[132] Patterson v. New York, 432 U.S. 197, 209 (1977).
[133] Liparota v. United States, 471 U.S. 419, 424 (1985) (citing United States v. Hudson, 11 U.S. 32, 7 Cranch 32, 3 L. Ed. 259 (1812)).

according to the *Patterson* logic, if a state chooses to include *mens rea* in the definition of an offense, it may take lesser steps of placing the burden of proof on the defendant because "greater power includes the lesser."[134] Accordingly, the *Patterson* logic promotes shifting all burdens of proof to the defendant.

Sixth, adopting the Canadian interpretation of the presumption of innocence is desirable given the utter disregard of the presumption of innocence by legislative bodies and courts alike.[135] For instance, the Terrorism Prosecution Act[136] allows the Attorney General or his/her highest-ranking subordinate to certify the existence of one of the essential elements of the offense, such as coercion or intimidation.[137] Upon certification, the prosecutor is not required to prove the certified essential element of the offense. If *Winship*[138] had been properly adjudicated, this statute would be unconstitutional, because it removes an essential fact of the offense from jury assessment and from the prosecution's burden of proof.

Finally, by implementing the Canadian approach, we would avoid problems with the concept of federalism by allowing the states to define their offenses as they see fit, while requiring the states to prove every fact necessary to convict or to enhance punishment.[139] The states would be free to label a fact as an element of the offense, an excuse, justification, sentencing factor, or whatever else, so long as the defendant is not required to prove *anything*.

D. THE QUANTUM OF PROOF

The second central concept implied in "beyond a reasonable doubt" is the degree of proof—the quantum—required for conviction. This concept is more

---

[134] Patterson v. New York, 432 U.S. 197, 209 (1977).

[135] Although the United States Supreme Court in Sandstrom v. Montana, 442 U.S. 510 (1979), decisively prohibited the use of the presumption that relives the persecution of the burden of proving mental state by requiring an inference of the existence of criminal intent from the fact of criminal conduct, some courts turned a blind eye to the Sandstrom judgment by allowing mandatory presumption of intent identical to the one invalidated in Sandstrom. *See* State v. Caldwell 607 N.E.2d 1096(Ohio. 1992).

[136] 18 USCS § 2332 (2001).

[137] 18 USCS § 2332 (2001), subsection (d) states: "(d) Limitation on prosecution. No prosecution for any offense described in this section shall be undertaken by the United States except on written certification of the Attorney General or the highest ranking subordinate of the Attorney General with responsibility for criminal prosecutions that, in the judgment of the certifying official, such offense was intended to coerce, intimidate, or retaliate against a government or a civilian population."

[138] Winship, 397 U.S. 358 (1970).

[139] *See* Jones v. United States, 526 U.S. 227; 119 S. Ct. 1215; 143 L. Ed. 2d 311 (1999)(The court concluded that the state legislature is not constrained to identify the facts relevant to the punishment or to establish fixed penalties, but the U.S. Supreme Court will review the procedures by which the facts that raise the possible penalty are to be given, who must find facts, and what burden must be satisfied to demonstrate them.).

problematic than the presumption of innocence. The history of the standard of proof in criminal trials does not explain the quantum of proof. It is merely described as having a satisfied conscience[140] to convict or just cause to acquit.[141]

The United States Supreme Court in *Winship* concluded that the standard of proof "impresses on the trier of fact the necessity of reaching a *subjective state of certitude* of the facts in issue." In *Jackson v. Virginia*,[142] the Court slightly modified the test to "impress upon the fact finder the need to reach a subjective state of *near certitude* of guilt of the accused."[143] This test is slightly less rigorous than the *Winship* formulation. The phrase "subjective state of certitude/near certitude" is fairly similar to the ancient definition "satisfied conscience" stated in Bracton's. Each phrase refers to a subjective state of mind of a juror sufficient to render a conviction. Yet, the English courts after approving "beyond a reasonable doubt" as a necessity in criminal trials[144] realized the unusual difficulties in defining that phrase. Consequently, they adopted a very similar standard of proof: "[Y]ou must not convict unless you are satisfied."[145] These analogous standards are intended to escape from a *quantitative* standard of proof by introducing a *qualitative standard,* one that focuses on the jurors' subjective state of mind.

However, scholars tend to be aggressive in defending a qualitative standard of proof. Professor Kaplan offered two rationales to explain why "beyond a reasonable doubt" is not quantitative. First, any quantitative standard admits a percentage of error. If we told the jury that they must be 99 percent sure of guilt, we would be telling them that one innocent defendant will be found guilty per 100 cases. We refrain from admitting that we allow conviction of the innocent. Second, the jury should consider the advantages and disadvantages of convicting the defendant. It is far less serious for society to acquit an embezzler than to acquit a child molester. Therefore, the qualitative standard offers flexibility in decision making that is necessary for many considerations such as the danger of repetition for a child molester.[146]

Another article defending the qualitative standard of proof suggests that we should not explain the literal meaning of "beyond a reasonable doubt";

---

[140] 2 BRACTON, ON THE LAWS AND CUSTOMS OF ENGLAND, OF PLEA OF THE CROWN 405 (Samuel E. Thorne ed., Harvard University Press 1968).
[141] SIR MATTHEW HALE, THE HISTORY OF THE COMMON LAW OF ENGLAND, 346 (6th ed., Henry Butterworth, law-bookseller 1820).
[142] Jackson v. Virginia, 443 U.S. 307, 315 (1979).
[143] *Id.* at 315.
[144] Woolmington v. Director of Public Prosecutions, [1935] App. Cas. 462 (H.L.).
[145] *See* Regina v. Summers [1952] 1 ALL E.R. 1059; (1952) 36 Crim. App. R. 14 (The court of criminal appeals in England has suggested that the judge in summing up should not make use of the expression "reasonable doubt"; it is far better to say to the jury "you must not convict unless you are satisfied by the evidence given by the prosecutor that the offense has been committed."). *See also* Walters v. Regina [1969] 2 App. Cas.26,30 (The standard, "satisfied so that they are sure," was approved by the privy counsel).
[146] John Kaplan, *Decision Theory and the Factfinding Process*, 20 Stan. L. Rev. 1065, 1073-1074 (1968).

rather, we should focus jury attention on the process of reaching the state of mind that justifies the conviction.[147]

The arguments in these articles and similar arguments elsewhere[148] carry some validity, since the standard of proof is truly difficult to quantify. However, these arguments are misleading because they shift our attention from the highest degree of certainty required for conviction to a concept dependent entirely on the subjective state of mind of a juror, which varies from the highest degree of certainty to the lowest one. These arguments provide a safe harbor for erroneous instructions because they shift the duty of ensuring that the jury understands the appropriate quantum of proof from the trial judge to the jury, who then applies a *subjective* quantum of proof. These arguments, simply, license the jurors to determine the quantum of proof according to their subjective state of mind under the label of "beyond a reasonable doubt."

Some English courts adopted the standard of "feel sure of guilt" as an alternative to the "beyond a reasonable doubt" formula.[149] This new standard of proof was embraced because of the difficulty of explaining the qualifying adjective, "reasonable," in "beyond a reasonable doubt" instructions.[150]

"Feel sure of guilt" is considerably superior to other explanations of "beyond a reasonable doubt" because it uses clear, commonplace language and indicates that a high degree of certainty is required for conviction.

However, empirical research shows that the "satisfied so that one feels sure" approach can make it almost impossible to get a conviction. If 100 percent certainty is required to convict, convictions disappear from the realm of the metaphysically possible.[151] The result of this research was astonishing to the legal profession in England, which called for wider empirical research, using the general public to represent mock jurors and magistrate judges.[152] Both groups were given instructions similar to the ones in the *Ferguson* case.[153] The result of

---

[147] Paul C. Smith, *The Process of Reasonable Doubt: A Proposed Instruction in Response to Victor v. Nebraska*, 41 Wayne L. Rev. 1811 (1995).

[148] *See* Charles R. Nesson, *Reasonable Doubt and Permissive Inferences: The Value of Complexity*, 92 Harv. L .Rev. 1187, 1192-99 (1979).

[149] The Privy Counsel in Jackson v. State, unreported, 29 October 1998, approved the "feel sure" formula.

[150] *See* Regina v. Hepworth & Fearnley [1955] 2 ALL E.R. 918; (1955) 39 Crim. App. R. 152(The court held, "it was very unfortunate to talk to juries about 'reasonable doubt' because the explanation given as to what is reasonable and what is not reasonable doubt are so very often extraordinarily difficult to follow and is very difficult to tell a jury what is reasonable doubt...one would be on safe ground if one said in a criminal case to a jury: 'you must be satisfied beyond a reasonable doubt' and one could also say 'you the jury must be completely satisfied' or better still: 'you must feel sure of the prisoner's guilt.'").

[151] John Warwick Montgomery, *The Criminal Standard of Proof*, 148 New L. J.582 (1998).

[152] Michael Zander, *The Criminal Standard of Proof—How Sure is Sure?*, 150 New L. J. 1517 (2000).

[153] *See* Ferguson v. The Queen [1979] 1 ALL E.R. 877(The privy counsel held, "it is generally sufficient and safe to direct a jury that they must be satisfied beyond reasonable

this research was even more surprising. Fifty-one percent of the "general public" group required themselves to be 100 percent sure before conviction, while 31 percent of the "magistrate judges" groups required themselves to be 100 percent sure before conviction. What is more surprising is that three-quarters of both the general public and magistrate judges required themselves to be 90 percent sure before conviction.

The benefits of the "feel sure" formula are undeniable, but the cost of adopting this formula is excessive. It raises the degree of certainty required for conviction to allow unwarranted acquittals. If unwarranted acquittals became common, it would encourage substantial disregard of the law.[154] The public would demand more severe punishment for those who were found guilty. Therefore, unwarranted acquittals could result in a harsher justice system.[155]

The only viable method for satisfactorily defining the quantum of proof is to group the concepts we intend to convey to the jury and express them fully in the jury instruction. These concepts are as follows.

First, the intended standard of proof is applicable to the criminal defendant when the judgment that ought to be rendered constitutes a moral stigma.[156] This concept is helpful to set the boundaries for the heavy burden of proof in criminal trials and to exclude the intended burden of proof in noncriminal trials such as civil commitment.[157]

Second, the criminal standard of proof is the highest because life or liberty is at stake.[158] The fact finder cannot know for certain what has occurred.[159] Therefore, there is some risk of error in decision making.[160] We

---

doubt so that they feel sure of the defendant's guilt. Nevertheless, other words will suffice, so long as the message is clear.").

[154] Stirland v. Director of Public Prosecutions [1944] App. Cas. 315, 324. (Lord Viscount Simon concluded, "A miscarriage of justice may arise from the acquittal of the guilty no less than from the conviction of the innocent.")

[155] GLANVILLE WILLIAMS, THE PROOF OF GUILT 157 (2d ed. 1958).

[156] Winship, 397 U.S. 358, 363 (1970). Some English courts offered identical rationales to the one mentioned in Winship. The courts rely on "moral blameworthiness of the accused." If the fact to be proven related to the moral blameworthiness of the accused, the State must prove this fact beyond reasonable doubt. *See, e.g.*, Regina v. Lambert [2001] 3 W.L.R. 206.(judgment by Lord Steyn)

[157] Addington v. Texas, 441 U.S. 418(1979).

[158] Winship, 397 U.S. 358, 363 (1970) (holding that "The accused during a criminal prosecution has at stake interests of immense importance, both because of the possibility that he may lose his liberty upon conviction and because of the certainty that he would be stigmatized by the conviction.").

[159] Winship, 397 U.S at 370 (1970) (Justice Harlan in a concurring opinion stated "[In] a judicial proceeding in which there is a dispute about the facts of some earlier event, the fact finder cannot acquire unassailably accurate knowledge of what happened.").

[160] Mathews v. Aldridge, 424 U.S.319, 344 (1976)(concluding that "Standards of proof, like other procedural due process rules are shaped by the risk of error inherent in the truthfinding process as applied to the generality of cases, not the rare exceptions.").

have to minimize the risk of error,[161] since the interest of the defendant is of such magnitude; therefore, society almost places the risk of error upon itself.[162]

Third, the prosecution is not required to prove the facts alleged to an absolute or mathematical certainty because such a measure of proof is often impossible in human affairs.[163] Adopting a standard of proof that requires almost absolute certainty, like "feel sure to convict," would frustrate police work[164] and generate undesirable consequences, as explained earlier.

Fourth, the standard of proof in criminal trials is said to be higher than the standard of "clear and convincing evidence."[165] The definition of "clear and convincing evidence" provided by the United States Supreme Court is flawed. The Court in *Santosky v. Kramer*[166] defined it as "adequately conveys to the fact finder the level of subjective certainty about his factual conclusion necessary to satisfy Due Process."[167] The problem with this definition is the vague, elastic concept of subjective certainty that the court used interchangeably to label the "beyond a reasonable doubt" and "clear and convincing" standards of proof. Indeed, it is very difficult to see any difference between the definition of "clear and convincing evidence" mentioned in *Santosky* and the definition of the higher standard of proof, "beyond a reasonable doubt," in *Winship*[168] and in *Jackson v. Virginia.*[169] However, the central criticism is limited to the overwhelming subjectivity of the phrase "subjective certainty," discussed earlier.

The New Jersey Supreme Court submitted a comprehensible definition of "clear and convincing evidence" for jury instructions that deserves endorsement. The court held that "clear and convincing evidence" "should produce in the mind of the trier of fact a firm belief or conviction as to the truth of the allegations sought to be established."[170]

The purpose of the fourth concept is to compare the intermediate standard of proof and the highest standard of proof. This strategy of explanation by comparison was used by many courts to explain the source of their doubts

---

[161] Greenholtz v. Nebraska Penal Inmates, 442 U.S. 1, 13 (1979) (holding that "The function of legal process, as that concept is embodied in the Constitution, and in the realm of factfinding, is to minimize the risk of erroneous decisions.").
[162] Addington v. Texas, 441 U.S. 418, 423-424 (1979).
[163] U.S v. Farina, 184 F. 2d 18, 20 (2d Cir. 1950).
[164] GLANVILLE WILLIAMS, THE PROOF OF GUILT 157 (2d ed. 1958).
[165] *See* Addington v. Texas, 441 U.S. 418 (1979).
[166] Santosky v. Kramer, 455 U.S. 745 (1982).
[167] *Id.* at 769.
[168] Winship, 397 U.S. 358 (1970).
[169] Jackson v. Virginia, 443 U.S. 307 (1979).
[170] Aiello v. Knoll Golf Club, 64 N.J. Super. 156, 162 (1960). *See also In re* Jobs, 108 N.J. 394, 407 (1987)(clear and convincing evidence standard of proof was defined as evidence that "produce[s] in the mind of the trier of fact a firm belief or conviction as to the truth of the allegations sought to be established, evidence so clear, direct and weighty and convincing as to enable [the factfinder] to come to a clear conviction, without hesitancy, of the truth of the precise facts in issue.").

regarding the "beyond a reasonable doubt" standard.[171] This strategy helps the jury to appreciate the nature of the highest degree of certainty required for conviction in criminal trials.[172]

Fifth, the intended standard of proof requires the jury to examine the quality rather than the quantity of evidence.[173] The jury may base their decision upon one single piece of evidence and exclude the rest, if they believed that such piece of evidence is the cornerstone of the case. This rule was fully elaborated in Sir Mathew Hale's analysis[174] and is firmly rooted in common law jurisdictions, but it is often left unspoken and neglected by courts in jury instructions.

If these five concepts are properly and adequately conveyed to the jury, the particular label of the quantum of proof will not make much difference. The courts may use the "beyond a reasonable doubt" phrase as in *Winship*[175] or the "evidential certainty" phrase suggested in *Cage.*[176] However, the label should not be as misleading as "moral certainty" or "beyond *substantial* doubt."[177]

V. SOME PRACTICAL CONSIDERATIONS

Identifying the elements of the standard of proof in criminal trials is not enough. We must ensure that such elements are properly and uniformly transmitted to the jury in light of the following practical considerations. First, the law requires the state to prove every fact necessary to prove the offense beyond a reasonable doubt.[178] Empirical studies show that the prosecution usually "wraps up" the case in the closing argument by telling the jury a story explaining the facts of the crime and possible motives of the defendant.[179] The result of this practice is to shift the burden of proof to the defendant, since he or she must offer a

---

171 *See* United States v. Isaac, 134 F. 3d 199, 202 (3d Cir. 1998)(holding that "it is not a mere possible or imaginary doubt, because as you well know, everything relating to human affairs and depending on oral testimony, is open to some possible or imaginary doubt."). *See also* State v. Taylor, 687 A. 2d 489, 502 (1996).

172 Winship, 397 U.S. 358, 369-370 (1970)(Justice Harlan's concurring opinion: "Even though the labels used for alternative standards of proof are vague and not very sure guides to decision making, the choice of the standard for a particular variety of adjudication does, I think, reflect a very fundamental assessment of the comparative social costs of erroneous factual determinations.").

173 *Compare* Santosky v. Kramer, 445 U.S. 745, 764 (1982) (holding that "fair preponderance of evidence is a standard of proof that by its very terms demands consideration of the quantity, rather than the quality.").

174 SIR MATTHEW HALE, THE HISTORY OF THE COMMON LAW OF ENGLAND 346 (6th ed., Henry Butterworth, law-bookseller 1820).

175 Winship, 397 U.S. 358 (1970).

176 Cage v. Louisiana, 498 U.S. 39, 41(1990).

177 Both phrases, "substantial doubt" and "moral certainty," were erroneously allowed in Victor v. Nebraska, 511 U.S. 1(1994).

178 Winship, 397 U.S. 358(1970).

179 Lawrence M. Solan, *Refocusing the Burden of Proof in Criminal Cases: Some Doubt About Reasonable Doubt,* 78 Tex. L. Rev. 105, 119-127(1999).

reasonable alternative to the scenario offered by the prosecutor. To avoid this problem the trial judge must:

1. Tell the jury that the law requires the state to prove the elements of the offense "beyond a reasonable doubt," and then explain that phrase.
2. *Enumerate those elements,* and the elements of the affirmative defenses that the state must disprove.
3. Ask the jury to make a factual determination based only on the elements the state has proved or failed to disprove.

Normally the trial judge informs the jury that the state bears the burden of proof. However, the key procedure in my proposal is the enumeration of the elements of the offense(s).[180] This procedure compels the prosecutor to establish the necessary facts; otherwise he fails to prove his case. It also prevents the prosecution from "wrapping up" the case by telling his alleged story and thus escaping from establishing one or more of the necessary facts.

There is another rationale supporting these procedures. It can be summarized as follows:

1. The jury does not give reasons for a guilty verdict. Therefore, the morality, legality, and basis of its decision cannot be reviewed.[181] The courts had two reasons for protecting the jury from such review: "[o]n the one hand it is in order to secure the finality of decisions arrived at by the jury, and on the other to protect the jurymen themselves and prevent their being exposed to pressure to explain the reasons which actuated them in arriving at their verdict."[182]
2. The jury, as a captive audience in an adversarial proceeding, cannot solicit information and thus is entirely dependent on the opposing parties to provide information.[183] When it applies inferential reasoning to the facts, inconsistent and incomprehensible evidence may result.
3. According to prevailing psychological jury decision-making theory, the jury attempts to construct the evidence into a coherent story that is consistent with the facts and makes sense given the members' existing knowledge.[184] The jury considers decision

---

[180]Some states adopted this strategy of spelling out the elements of the offense to the jury; See WISCONSIN JURY INSTRUCTIONS, 2 Wis. JI- Criminal instructions No. 1000-1195(2001).

[181] S. Shaun Nakatsuru, *Book Review: A Theory of the Trial of Robert P. Burns*, 50 U. Tornoto.L.J.363, 369 (2000).

[182]Regina . v. Thompson, (1961) 46 Crim. App. R. 72.

[183] Neil Vidmar, Shari Seidman Diamond, *Juries and Expert Evidence*, 66 Brook. L.Rev.1121,1134 (2001)

[184] Reid Hastie, *The Rule of "Stories" in Civil Jury Judgment*, 32 U. Mich. J. L. Reform 227, 229-233 (1999). *See also* REID HASTIE et al., INSIDE THE JURY (1983).

> alternatives (verdicts) by learning their attributes or elements.[185] It reaches a decision through the classification of a story into the best-fitting verdict category.[186]

Because the jurors are not required to reveal the reasoning underlying the verdict, and they are confronted with inconsistent information, they select the evidence that best fits their theory of the case. Throughout this process, the jurors may not realize that the evidence underlying their verdict must be proved beyond a reasonable doubt. They may accept evidence because it fits their theory of the case, even though it did not meet the required standard of proof. The role of the procedures I propose is to draw the jury's attention to the fact that they should consider only evidence that meets the standard of proof. Moreover, these procedures facilitate the decision-making process by providing a two-step rational analysis of conflicting evidence: first isolate the evidence proved beyond a reasonable doubt; then determine the facts at issue based upon this evidence alone.

We must give the issue of burden of proof more attention than it gets now. Less than half of the states in this country recommend giving a burden of proof instruction in their pattern jury instructions. Even the states that adopted pattern jury instructions implemented them only as recommendations. Many judges continue to give individualized instructions. I believe that transmitting the law clearly and correctly to juries is just as important as interpreting it properly..

The United States Supreme Court has sent mixed, confusing messages regarding jury instructions on burden of proof. In *Weeks v. Angelone*,[187] the Supreme Court decided by a narrow margin that a trial judge who presides over a death penalty case is not obliged to clear up the jury's confusion over a crucial sentencing instruction by doing more than pointing to the controlling language of the instructions.[188] Chief Justice Rehnquist concluded that it can be presumed that jurors understand their instructions.[189] On the other hand, that court in *Jackson v. Virginia*[190] concluded that "the *Winship* doctrine requires more than trial ritual."[191] This approach suggests that "beyond a reasonable doubt" instruction requires an explanation.

However, the *Apprendi*[192] decision asserted that sentencing factors are within the *Winship* limits and that they must be assessed by the jury and proven beyond a reasonable doubt. The decision incorporated the sentencing factors into the "beyond a reasonable doubt" instruction. Therefore, both the sentencing factors and "beyond a reasonable doubt" should be explained to the jury. The

---

185 *Id.*
186 *Id.*
187 Weeks v. Angelone, 528 U.S. 225(2000).
188 *Id.* at 227.
189 *Id.* at 234.
190 Jackson v. Virginia, 443 U.S. 307 (1979).
191 *Id.* at 316-318.
192 Apprendi v. New Jersey, 530 U.S. 466 (2000).

alternative peculiar conclusion is that the standard of proof requires an explanation while the sentencing factors do not. That conclusion is unreasonable because it suggests that the standard of proof requires an explanation while the law that ought to be proven does not.

The paramount conclusion is that absent a plausible rationale for the presumption that the jury understands its instructions, I endorse the implication of the *Jackson* decision that "beyond a reasonable doubt" requires an explanation. Furthermore, this line of reasoning suggests that sentencing factors require an explanation, a suggestion implicitly overruling the *Weeks* decision as an indirect result of *Apprendi.*

Finally, since "beyond a reasonable doubt" is a constitutional requirement,[193] there must be uniform mandatory instructions regarding the standard of proof. The benefit of applying a uniform mandatory standard is not limited to definitional uniformity of an important doctrine nationally. It will eliminate inconsistent and confusing language in individualized jury instructions. Disfavored phrases such as "moral certainty" and "beyond substantial doubt"[194] will disappear and be replaced by accepted, comprehensible, uniform instructions.

The effect of inconsistent or confusing jury instructions on the standard of proof should not be underestimated. A juror who is confused or uncertain about the standard of proof may revert to a phrase like "moral certainty" because it has more appeal.

VI. CONCLUSION

The judge in the criminal trial must ensure that the applicable law is stated accurately and completely.[195] The trial judge's duty regarding the standard of proof in the criminal trial will be discharged if he or she states the two elements of the standard, namely, the presumption of innocence and the quantum of proof.

Regarding the presumption of innocence, there are two alternative interpretations. The existing United States Supreme Court interpretation requires the state to prove every fact that constitutes the offense and any fact that enhances the punishment, with the exception of recidivism as explained in *Winship and Apprendi.* However, the states may place the initial burden of proving the affirmative defenses on the defendant, as explained in *Patterson.* This initial burden operates as *a presumption* of guilt, which a defendant must overcome to shift the burden of disproving the defense to the state.[196] In other

---

[193] Winship, 397 U.S. 358 (1970).

[194] *See* Cage v. Louisiana, 498 U.S. 39 (1990), Victor v. Nebraska, 511 U.S. 1(1994).

[195] Sparf v. United States, 156 U.S. 51, 92 (1895).

[196] *See* Patterson v. New York, 432 U.S. 197,210 (1977)(Apparently, the Supreme Court does not recognize, as a practical effect, that placing the initial burden of proof in affirmative defenses on the defendant constitutes a presumption of guilt. The Court's

words, convicting a defendant in a criminal trial requires proving guilt. To prove guilt it is necessary to prove the offense(s) and disprove the defense(s). To place the initial burden of proving the defense(s) on the defendant is to create a presumption of guilt. It also means that if a defendant fails to satisfy the initial burden, he could be convicted despite the existence of a reasonable doubt in the mind of the trier of facts.

The proposed Canadian approach does not require the defendant to prove anything to avoid or to decrease the punishment; rather it requires the state to prove guilt by proving the elements of the offense and disproving defenses. In this case, no initial burden is placed on the defendant to prove his innocence; rather, the state bears the entire burden of proving *guilt*.

The Supreme Court's approach as explained in *Winship* and *Apprendi* is misleading because it diverts our attention from the presumption of innocence—which holds that the defendant is not required to prove *anything* because he is presumed innocent—to an entirely different perspective concerning the state's burden of proof in a criminal trial. Both concepts are relevant, but the Canadian approach is superior because it guards against the indirect shifting of any burden of proof to the defendant.

The quantum of proof in criminal trials is best explained by the five concepts stated in part IV (D) in this chapter. The burden of proof is a very heavy burden because life or liberty is at stake. The punishment constitutes a moral stigma. The state is not required to prove the facts alleged to absolute or mathematical certainty, but the burden is heavier than a firm belief or conviction as to the truth of the allegations sought to be established. The jurors must base their decision upon the quality of the evidence. Since they are the assessors of the credibility of the facts, they have discretion regarding what weight (including no weight) to give any evidence.

VII. PROPOSED JURY INSTRUCTIONS

The following instructions are based upon the discussion in part IV above. The trial judge should not only read the instructions to the jury, but should also provide a written copy of the instructions.[197] Because the standard of proof is the

---

view in Patterson is that the Due Process Clause only requires the most basic procedural safeguards to be observed. Accordingly, by pitting the interest of the accused against the social interest, the state is permitted to place the initial burden of proof on the accused in affirmative defenses.).

[197] *See* Geoffrey P. Kramer & Dorean M. Koenig, *Do Jurors Understand Criminal Jury Instructions? Analyzing the Results of the Michigan Juror Comprehension Project*, 23 U. Mich. J.L. Ref. 401, 428 (1990) (Empirical research shows that written instructions improve jurors' comprehension significantly.). *See also* JURY TRIAL INNOVATIONS (G. Thomas Munsterman et al. eds, 1997).

determining factor in the jury's assessment of the evidence, it must be explained to the jury both at the beginning and end of the trial.[198]

I offer two alternate jury instructions. The first adopts the Canadian approach, emphasizing the presumption of innocence, while the second reflects the existing American law as explained in Supreme Court decisions.

A. VERSION ONE (ADOPTING THE CANADIAN APPROACH)

The defendant is accused of committing (name of the offense(s)). You must know that the law presumes that he is innocent until proven guilty. This presumption never shifts the defendant. It will remain with the defendant from the commencement of the trial until the end. It means that the defendant is not required to prove anything. On the other hand, the state must prove every fact that constitutes the offense and disprove any fact that exonerates the defendant or reduces the punishment and that has been placed in issue. The facts that constitute the offense are called the "elements of the offense." Those elements are (state the elements of the offense(s) charged). You must not convict if any of these elements is absent. The defendant raised (if a defense or mitigating circumstances has been raised) the defense of (name of the defense raised). The defendant is not required to prove the existence of the defense (or the mitigating circumstances). The state is required to prove the absence of the facts that constitute the defense. These facts are (state the facts that constitute the defense). If the state disproves the existence of *any* fact constituting the defense (or mitigating circumstances) and proves the existence of *every* fact constituting the offense(s) you must convict. If the state fails to prove the existence of *any* fact constituting the offense(s) or fails to disprove the existence of *any* fact constituting the defense you must acquit.[199]

The state must prove every fact that constitutes the offense(s) and disprove every fact that constitutes the defense (or the mitigating circumstances) and that has been placed in issue by the evidence beyond a reasonable doubt (or to evidential certainty). This burden of proof is a heavy burden because the life or liberty of the defendant is at stake and the conviction constitutes a moral stigma. The state is not required to prove the facts alleged to absolute or mathematical certainty because there are very few things in life that can be proven to absolute certainty. If we required the state to prove its case to absolute certainty, no offender would go to jail and it would be an invitation to

---

198 Vicki L. Smith, *Impact of Pretrial Instruction on Jurors' Information Processing and Decision Making*, 76 J. App. Psychol. 220 (1991) (Empirical research has revealed that jurors instructed both before and after the evidence are better able to integrate facts and law than jurors instructed only after the evidence is presented).

199 *See* JURY TRIAL INNOVATIONS (G. Thomas Munsterman et al. eds., 1997) (Juror comprehension of the instructions will be improved by using alternative phrases leading to the same meaning.).

lawlessness and disorder. Before you convict you must be convinced of guilt at least to a degree higher than a firm belief of the truth of the allegations, but absolute certainty is not required. If we allowed conviction for a degree of certainty such as a mere firm belief in the allegations, many innocent defendants would go to jail. You should found your decision upon the quality of the evidence alone. You are free to ignore any evidence if you are not satisfied as to its credibility. You may consider any evidence if you are satisfied as to its credibility.

B. VERSION TWO (REFLECTING THE EXISTING LAW)

The defendant is accused of committing (name of the offense(s)). You must know that law presumes that he is innocent until proven guilty. This presumption never shifts the defendant. It will remain with the defendant from the commencement of the trial until the end. It means that the state must prove every fact that constitutes the offense and disprove any affirmative defense that exonerates the defendant or reduces the punishment. The facts that constitute the offense are called the "elements of the offense." Those elements are (state the elements of the offense(s) charged). You must not convict if any of these elements is absent. The defendant raised (if a defense or mitigating circumstances has been raised) the defense of (name of the defense raised). *If* the defense(s) raised is an affirmative defense(s), the following must be added: "The defendant is required to prove the existence of the defense by a preponderance of evidence (or whatever degree of certainty is required), which means that the facts he/she alleged are more probable than not. The state is required to prove the absence of the facts that constitute the defense. These facts are (state the facts that constitute the defense). If the state disproves the existence of *any* fact constituting the defense (or mitigating circumstances) and proves the existence of *every* fact constituting the offense(s), you must convict. If the state fails to prove the existence of *any* fact constituting the offense(s) or fails to disprove the existence of *any* fact constituting the defense, you must acquit.[200]

The state must prove every fact that constitutes the offense(s) and disprove every fact that constitutes the defense (or the mitigating circumstances) "beyond a reasonable doubt" (or to evidential certainty). This burden of proof is a heavy burden because the life or liberty of the defendant is at stake and the conviction constitutes a moral stigma. The state is not required to prove the facts alleged to absolute or mathematical certainty because there are very few things in life that can be proven to absolute certainty. If we required the state to prove its case to absolute certainty, no offender would go to jail and it would be an invitation to lawlessness and disorder. Before you convict you must be convinced of guilt at least to a degree higher than a firm belief in the truth of the allegations, but absolute certainty is not required. If we allowed conviction for a degree of certainty such as a mere firm belief in the allegations, many innocent

[200] *Id.*

defendants would go to jail. You should found your decision upon the quality of the evidence alone. You are at large to ignore any evidence if you are not satisfied as to its credibility. You may consider any evidence if you are satisfied as to its credibility.

Chapter Two

Reconstructing Reasonableness in Criminal Law*

I. INTRODUCTION

The concept of reasonableness or of the "reasonable person" has become one of the central cornerstones in criminal law. It has been introduced into the elements of several offenses[201] and defenses.[202] Some jurisdictions define it as an average, ordinary person who is a representative of the general community;[203] others are silent and leave it to the jury to define as desired. Therefore, it is desirable to explore the origins and objectives of the concept of reasonableness and examine the success of achieving such objectives.

This chapter proposes reconstructing the concept of reasonableness as a rule of evidence as opposed to a rule of substance. Considering the "reasonable person" concept as a permissive inference or a mandatory presumption seems well suited to the rules of evidence because its ability to accomplish the objectives and policies underlie the concept of reasonableness. This chapter avoids the temptation of discussing the concept of reasonableness within a particular offense or defense. Instead, this chapter isolates the concept from the

---

* Reprinted from volume 29 issue # 2 of the journal of legislation with the permission of the journal.

[201] *See* Alabama Criminal Code, Code of Ala. § 13A-2-2 .3 (2001) (inducing the concept of reasonableness into negligence); Delaware Criminal Code, 11 Del. C. § 307 (2001) (inducing the concept of reasonableness into intention, recklessness, knowledge or belief).

[202] *See* Delaware Criminal Code, 11 Del. C. § 431 (2001) (inducing the concept of reasonableness into defense of duress); Arizona Criminal code (A.R.S. § 13-404 (2001) (inducing the concept of reasonableness into self defense); Illinois Criminal Code § 720 ILCS 5/9-2(b) (inducing the concept of reasonableness into defense of provocation).

[203] *See* Bedder v. D.P.P [1954] 1 WLR 1119, See also people v. Day, 2 Cal. Rptr. 2d 916, 912-922(Cal.Ct.App.1992)

zone of particular defenses or offenses while discussing the common foundation of the concept shared by every offense and defense.

Part II of this chapter traces the roots of the concept of reasonableness, the factors that shaped it and its development by courts and legislators. Part III explains the policies that underlie the reasonable person standard. Part IV attributes the failure of achieving the goals of the reasonableness standard to the current practice of considering reasonableness as a rule of substance. Part V argues for an expansive view of construing reasonableness as a rule of evidence that incorporates the *genuine* objectives of reasonableness. Part VI clarifies the underpinnings of presumptions and inferences in criminal law. It proposes constructing reasonableness as presumption or an inference, which is the best application of the rules of evidence to the concept of reasonableness. Part VII concludes that the concept of reasonableness should be construed as a rule of evidence. Part VIII proposes alternative jury instructions for the concept of reasonableness as mandatory presumption or as permissive inference. It offers courts and legislatures the choice of two alternative rules of evidence based upon the weight of the burden that the defendant bears to overcome the evidential rule of reasonableness. If reasonableness is construed as a mandatory presumption, the defendant bears a greater burden than if reasonableness is construed as a permissive inference. The proposal in this chapter is suitable for all offenses and defenses in criminal law because of the generality of the discussion.

II. THE RISE AND FALL OF REASONABLENESS IN CRIMINAL LAW

One of the historical cornerstones in criminal liability is the maxim "*actus non facit reum nisi mens sit rea.*"[204] This maxim states that an individual cannot be convicted of a criminal offense unless he had a guilty mind while committing the prohibited act. This cardinal rule is a purely subjective test of liability that has dominated the legal analysis since the Bracton era.[205] For instance, Blackstone in his analysis of provocation defense did not make any reference to objective liability or its application of reasonableness. He considered the mere pulling of the deceased's nose or other acts of indignity as sufficient

---

[204] JAMES FITZJAMES STEPHEN, 2 HISTORY OF THE CRIMINAL LAW OF ENGLAND 94 (LONDON, MACMILLAN 1883).

[205] The issue of subjective mental state was the core of liability. *See* 2 BRACTON ON THE LAWS AND CUSTOMS OF ENGLAND 340-342(SAMUEL E. THORNE ed., Harvard University press 1968); historically malice was clearly understood to have subjective meaning involving an act wrongfully directed at the victim; See Jeremy Horder, *Two Histories And Four Hidden Principals Of Mens Rea* ,113 L.Q.Rev.95 (1997)

provocation.[206] The subjective liability approach emerges from the notion that individuals have the power to choose their actions and should be liable only for the misuse of their power.[207]

In the early nineteenth century, the language of reasonableness appeared in East's writings on the provocation defense. However, the question of reasonableness was limited to the gravity of the provocation or to the time elapsed between the provocative acts and the homicide.[208] Shortly thereafter, by the mid-nineteenth century, some courts departed from the traditional subjective liability standard by ignoring the actual mental state of the defendant.[209] The test of a "reasonable and ordinary person" was implanted in the landmark case of *Regina v. Welsh.*[210] The standard of a reasonable and ordinary person was mentioned only as a method of explaining the law of provocation to the jury.[211] Although this case utilized some objective elements in assessing adequate provocation, it was never intended to abrogate the subjective characteristics of the defense or to employ a new standard of liability.[212]

Ultimately, three factors shaped the courts' decisions by the end of the nineteenth century and the beginning of the twentieth century: (1) historical subjective liability; (2) the emergence of objective liability; and (3) inadvertent statement of the standard of reasonableness.

Perusing these factors, the courts struggled to formulate a satisfactory standard of reasonableness. Some courts adopted a purely objective standard of reasonableness,[213] while others diluted its harshness by infusing some subjective

---

[206] WILLIAM BLACKSTONE, 4 COMMENTARIES ON THE LAW OF ENGLAND 190 (13th ed., London, A. Strahan 1800)

[207] Lord Simon concedes: "the general basis for criminal responsibility is the power of choice involved in the axiomatic freedom of the human being." Lynch v. D.P.P [1975] 1 ALL. E.R. 913

[208] EDWARD HYDE EAST, 1 TREATISE OF THE PLEAS OF THE CROWN 232-255 (London, A. Strahan 1803)

[209] *See* Regina v. Woodrow, 15 M. & W 404,153.Eng.Rep. 907(1846); Regina v. Stephens, [1865-1866] 1 Q.B 702.

[210] Regina v. Welsh, 11 Cox CC 336 (1869)

[211] *Id.*; *see also* Lord Hoffmann in Regina v. Smith (Morgan), [2001] 1 AC 146, [2000] 4 All ER 289, [2000] 3 WLR 654.

[212] Although the "reasonable and prudent person" standard was introduced in 1869 in Welsh, Stephen did not consider the rule established as rule in the common law of England in 1883. It was first proposed as the standard of the ordinary person by Criminal Law Commission of 1878-1879. JAMES FITZJAMES STEPHEN, 3 HISTORY OF THE CRIMINAL LAW OF ENGLAND 79-81(London, Macmillan 1883)

[213] Bedder v. D.P.P [1954] 1 WLR 1119 (ignoring any unusual physical characteristics of the accused for the purpose of the "reasonable person" test). *See also* people v. Day, 2 Cal. Rptr. 2d 916, 912-922(Cal. Ct. App. 1992) (insisting that a defendant's belief is reasonable if and only if the hypothetical reasonable person would have held a similar belief).

elements into the "reasonable person" standard.[214] The courts that adopted the hybrid subjective/objective standard of reasonableness were faced with the problem of choosing which subjective elements should be induced into reasonableness to be considered by the jury. A subjective element of psychiatric evidence of a mental condition of the defendant was accepted by some courts,[215] while it was rejected by others.[216] The inconsistencies of the courts' decisions arose primarily from competing theories of objective and subjective liability.

Reasonableness as a species of objective liability was designed to eliminate the indeterminacy of subjective liability. It aimed to impose a rule of law preventing defendants from escaping liability by setting their own standard under the subjective liability label.[217] Concerns with such indeterminacy were voiced by the courts on many occasions.[218] Although these concerns have merit,

---

[214] People v. Mathews, 30 Cal.Rptr.2d 330,335(Cal.Ct.App.1994) (affirming that a blind and hearing-impaired defendant claiming self-defense was entitled to be held to the standard of reasonable blind and hearing-impaired person as opposed to that of a reasonable person with normal eyesight and hearing); Gentry v. State, 441 S.E.E.2d 249, 250 (Ga. Ct. App 1994) (concluding that the "reasonable person" standard should be measured against those of the reasonable woman); Rodriguez v. State, 641 S.W.2d 669,672 (Tex. Ct. App. 1982) (upholding that the relative weight, size, and strength of a defendant claiming self-defense compared with that of his victim are matters that may be considered in determining the reasonableness of the defendant's actions); State v. Wanrow, 559 P.2d 548(Wash.1977)("reasonable person" does not mean reasonable male, it should mean reasonable woman when the defendant is a female).

[215] R v. Smith (Morgan), [2001] 1 AC 146, [2000] 4 All ER 289, [2000] 3 WLR 654.

[216] People v. Pecora, 107 Ill. App. 2d 283; 246 N.E.2d 865 (1969) (holding that the religious believes and the mental disturbance of a defendant are irrelevant).

[217] Lauren E. Goldman, Non Confrontational Killing And The Appropriate Use Of Battered Child Syndrome Testimony: The Hazards Of Subjective Self-Defense And The Merits Of Partial Excuses 45 Case W. Res. L. Rev. 185, 208(1994). Goldman argues that the subjectivity of self-defense would "infringe on the premise of our criminal law system that the preservation of life is an important value and that the taking of a life will be exempt from criminality and punishment only in a narrow, societal-determined set of circumstances" *Id.*

[218] In Smith [Morgan] Lord Slynn concluded that (It is thus not enough for the accused to say "I am a depressive; therefore I cannot be expected to exercise control." The jury must ask whether he has exercised the degree of self-control to be expected of someone in his situation) R v. Smith (Morgan), [2001] 1 AC 146, [2000] 4 All ER 289, [2000] 3 WLR 654

People v. Goetz held:

> We cannot allow the perpetrator of serious crime to go free simply because that person believed his action were reasonable and necessary to prevent some perceived harm. To completely exonerate…an individual, no matter how aberrational or bizarre his thought patterns, would allow citizens to set their own standards for the permissible use of force. It would also allow a legally competent defendant suffering from delusions to kill or perform act of violence with impunity, contrary to fundamental principles of justices and criminal law.

they are troubled by some practical considerations. The courts initially realized, on the basis of fairness, that particular subjective traits of the defendant that distinguish him from the general community[219] ought to be considered by a jury.[220] Subsequently, some courts realized that they should recognize all the particular characteristics of a defendant,[221]so long as they were not mere unfounded allegations of subjectiveness or futile excuses,[222] because any proposed distinction between the characteristics would be an arbitrary one.[223] The view was that to infuse into the objective test subjective factors, such as immaturity, is to recognize its effect on the defendant's decision-making process. So why should a court not recognize that other factors, such as serious clinical depression, affect the defendant's decision-making process?[224]

Courts that resisted accepting personal characteristics were motivated by a fear that introducing every subjective unique characteristic of the defendant into the reasonableness standard would eventually destroy the objectivity of the standard.[225] Most importantly, this would frustrate the function of objectivity, which protects society from unjustifiable, unexpected behavior. Furthermore, it was suggested that the standard of reasonableness must "possess some generality; a standard hewn to the unique attributes of each person would be no standard."[226]

Those who introduce only selective subjective elements into the reasonable person standard lack criteria for the selection. Indisputably, some subjective traits, such as bad temper, envy, or greed, should not considered by the jury. However, for practical considerations, a list of acceptable and nonacceptable subjective traits is not available. The jury can perform this task efficiently by striking the balance between acceptable and nonacceptable subjective elements, as representative of social moral norms. However, the implication of an "open-door policy" for the subjective elements or personal

---

People v. Goetz, 497 N.E.2d 41, 50 (N.Y.1986)

219 Regina v. Dincer [1983] VR 460

220 D.P.P v. Camplin [1978] AC 705, [1978] 2 All. E.R 168, [1978] 2 WLR 679, 67 Cr App Rep 14, 142 JP 320 (allowing the age of the defendant to be factor); State v. Kelly, 478 A.2d 364 (N.J.1984) (accepting the history of abuse in cases of battered women syndrome in the jury instructions); State v. Hundley, 693 P.2d 475,479(Kan.1985) (holding that a reasonable person in a case of battered woman defense is a reasonable prudent battered wife).

221 Lord Morris in D.P.P v. Camplin stated, "It would now be unreal to tell the jury that the notional 'reasonable man' is someone without the characteristics of the accused: it would be to intrude into their province" D.P.P v. Camplin [1978] AC 705, [1978] 2 All ER 168.

222 RICHARD SINGER & JOHN LA FOND, CRIMINAL LAW 53 (1997).

223 *See* Lord Slynn analysis in R v. Smith (Morgan), [2001] 1 AC 146, [2000] 4 All ER 289.

224 *Id.*

225 Robert Unikel, Comment, *"Reasonable" Doubt: A Critique of The Reasonable Woman Standard in American Jurisprudence*, 87 NW. U. L. Rev. 326,371 (1992)

226 GEORGE P. FLETCHER, RETHINKING CRIMINAL LAW 507 (1978)

characteristics of the defendant would destroy the foundation of reasonableness by eliminating the objectivity of the standard.

III. POLICIES THAT UNDERLIE THE REASONABLE PERSON STANDARD

Numerous objectives promote the reasonableness standard. A purely objective form of reasonableness proposes that public policy sacrifice the individual good for the general good.[227] The punishment does not depend on the moral blameworthiness of the defendant.[228] The tests of liability are external. A defendant is held liable to a reasonable prudent person standard even though he may be morally innocent because he has less than ordinary intelligence or prudence.[229] Individuals are a means to an end in that criminal law uses them to promote the general welfare by setting an example for others of the appropriate modes of conduct.[230]

A moderate perspective suggests that one of the prime rationales for the reasonableness standard is to protect individuals from unjustified threats and expose them to what they may expect from their fellow citizens.[231] Therefore, reasonableness is measured by the relationship between the victim and the defendant.[232] The extraordinary characteristics of the defendant are considered only if they were known or obvious to the victim.[233]

It has been argued that reasonableness represents the socially acceptable standard of conduct.[234] Reasonableness crystallizes the norms and

---

[227] O. W. HOLMES, THE COMMON LAW 48 (1881)

[228] *Id.* at 49, *See also* Commonwealth v. Stasko, 471 Pa. 373; 370 A.2d 350(Pa.1977) (The psychologist was introduced to testify concerning the appellant's tendency to have a short temper and erupt in sudden rages. The purpose of the testimony was to show that, in the case of this particular accused, there was sufficient provocation for the attack. This evidence was inadmissible since the court insisted that reasonableness is purely an objective standard.).

[229] *Id.* at 51. *See also* Commonwealth v. Kennedy 170 Masc., 20, 48 N.E. 770,777 (1897) (stating that "the aim of the law is not to punish sins, but is to prevent certain external results") (Holmes, J).

[230] GEORGE P. FLETCHER, RETHINKING CRIMINAL LAW 505-507 (1978).

[231] *See* Lord Diplock, D.P.P v. Camplin [1978] AC 705, [1978] 2 All ER 168, [1978] 2 WLR 679 (defining reasonable person to mean "an ordinary person of either sex, not exceptionally excitable or pugnacious, but possessed of such powers of self-control *as everyone is entitled to expect that his fellow citizens will exercise in society as it is today.*")

[232] ARTHUR RIPSTEIN, EQUALITY, RESPONSIBILITY, AND THE LAW 194-195(1999)

[233] *Id.*

[234] Martha Minow & Todd Rakoff, Is The "Reasonable Person" Reasonable Standard In Multicultural World? In Everyday Practices And Trouble Cases 48(Austin Sarat et al. eds., 1998)

values of the society and incorporates them into a set of rules that governs individuals' conduct and that communicates its meanings to the public frankly.[235] Conduct is deemed acceptable when it meets our social expectation. We expect individuals to control negative feelings of anger, jealousy, and greed.[236] If an individual fails to control such feelings there is no reason to award him deferential treatment or excuse his conduct.[237] By contrast, when a conduct is understandable and expected from a person in the defendant's situation because of particular trait or infirmity in human nature, such a person may be excused.[238]

In sum, the objectives of the standard of reasonableness are: (1) setting a standard of conduct manifesting the social moral norms; (2) educating the public as to the proper and acceptable standard of behavior; and (3) protecting individuals from unjustified conducts by exposing them only to expected behavior. The logical inquiry following this exposition of the objectives is: has the reasonableness standard achieved these objectives?

IV. THE FAILURE TO ACHIEVE THE OBJECTIVES OF THE REASONABLENESS STANDARD

The first objective of reasonableness is setting a standard of conduct manifesting the social moral norms. This objective per se is false because the standard of reasonableness ignores the uniqueness of an individual's behavior.[239] When the standard is strictly applied, it prevents the consideration of relevant circumstances particular to an individual case.[240] It has been truly said that "[an attempt to generalize a rule of conduct results in] losing variability, individuality and meaning and ending with deceptively low correlations that relate to mythical exemplar than any particular person."[241] By establishing an "average person" as our standard, we actually end up describing no person at all.

Reasonableness is a misleading concept. While some jurists believe that it establishes the boundary between acceptable and nonacceptable behavior,[242] in reality it is a flawed concept that opens the door for judges and

---

[235] *Id.*

[236] GEORGE P. FLETCHER, RETHINKING CRIMINAL LAW 514 (1978).

[237] *Id.*

[238] Regina v. Humphreys [1995] 4 ALL.ER 1008.

[239] Dolores A. Donovan & Stephanie M. Wildman, *Is Reasonable Man Obsolete? A Critical Prospective On Self Defense And Provocation*, 14 Loy. LA.L Rev 435, 462-467 (1981).

[240] *Id.*

[241] Norman J. Finkel, *Achilles Fuming, Odysseus Stewing, And Hamlet Brooding: On The Story Of The Murder /Manslaughter Distinction*, 74 Neb.L.Rev.742, 767(1995).

[242] Robert Unikel, Comment, *"Reasonable" Doubt: A Critique of The Reasonable Woman Standard in American Jurisprudence*, 87 NW. U. L. Rev. 326,329 (1992) ("the concept of 'reasonableness' effectively establishes the boundary between an acceptable

jury alike to import their own values, morals, and ideals into the definition of reasonableness.[243] To make matters worse, reasonableness indirectly invites the jurors to nullify the law by justifying the defendant's behavior when they believe that any reasonable person (including, perhaps, themselves) "would have acted similarly under the circumstances."[244]

The reasonable person standard stands as a barrier that precludes consideration of the unique characteristics of an individual defendant. For instance, if a defendant is from a minority group his cultural background will be ignored because the "reasonable person" standard reflects only the norms of the dominant culture and excludes the values of the other groups in society.[245] The problem materializes when a defendant from a different culture is denied the opportunity to explain why his actions were reasonable within the traditions of his culture.

The second objective of reasonableness is that the objectivity of the reasonable person standard manifests the cumulative moral sense of the community. It educates individuals as to the proper and acceptable standard of conduct within the community. Indeed, law can be educative by communicating to the public the proper standard of conduct. Petrazycki offers an excellent analysis of the educational function of law.[246] He explains that the law influences public behavior through the process of habit formation.[247] In this context, the acts required by the law influence the individuals who perform them.[248] The repetition of these acts promotes positive habits of doing and negative habits of abstaining.[249] Individual characters develop through the endorsing of positive good habits and the weakening of negative bad habits.[250] The law creates an impulsive propensity in the society to exercise beneficial habits and to refrain from harmful habits.[251]

---

exercise of individual freedom and an unacceptable inference with the rights of the others")

[243] John Perry, *Culpability, Mistake And official Interpretation of law*, 25 Am. J. Crim. L.1,27 (1997); *See also* IRWIN A. HOROWITZ & THOMAS E. WILLGING, THE PSYCHOLOGY OF LAW: INTEGRATION AND APPLICATIONS 73 (1984) ("Judges project rules of reason into their decisions by referring to the actions of a hypothetical 'reasonable person'....")

[244] Irwin A. Horowitz et al., *Jury Nullification Legal and Psychological perspectives*, 66 Brook.L.Rev.1207, 1209 (2001).

[245] *See* Richard Delgado, *Shadowboxing: An Essay On Power* ,77 Cornell L. Rev. 813,818(1992). *See also* William I. Torry, *The Doctrine of Provocation and The Reasonable Person Test: An Essay on Culture Theory and The Criminal Law*, 29 INT'L J.SOC.L. 1, 5- 6 (2001).

[246] LEON PETRAZYCKI, LAW AND MORALITY 301(Hugh W. Babb trans., Harvard University Press, 1955)

[247] *Id.*

[248] *Id.*

[249] *Id.*

[250] *Id.*

[251] *Id.*

The natural and logical question following acknowledgment of the educational function of law is whether implementing a reasonable person standard educates individuals. Consider this hypothesis. Conducts X, Y, and Z are prohibited. Individual A is punished for conduct X. Individual B is punished for conduct Y. Can A's and B's punishment be used to educate individuals C, D, and E? What if the conducts X, Y, and Z are vague concepts? If so, then punishing A and B will educate no one. In fact, it will have a negative effect. It will demoralize society because it would be punishing individuals for conducts they did not know were wrong or, at least, for conducts whose impropriety or illegality they were not able to fully comprehend. Reasonableness is not a specific act; it is an elastic concept containing an unlimited number of prohibitions. In straightforward terms, it is a vague criteria rather than a simple act. The educative function of law works efficiently with particular conducts such as homicide or larceny. Therefore, the message that is carried to the public by punishing the murderer is that killing is prohibited. Similarly, we punish for larceny because theft is prohibited. The situation is different with the reasonableness standard. We demand of individuals that they act reasonably. However, there is no rational definition of what constitutes reasonable conduct, and the courts do not agree on what acts are considered reasonable.[252]

Professor H.L.A. Hart rightly concluded that punishing innocent individuals for the sole purpose of advancing certain social objectives would generate massive adverse effects. It would produce a "state of general alarm and terror…if it were known that the innocent were likely to be seized and subjected to the pains of punishment [and might be] worse than any advance in security or social welfare brought about by these means could outweigh."[253]

The third objective of the reasonableness standard is the claim that the standard protects individuals from unjustified conducts by exposing them only to expected behavior.[254] Empirical research in the field of psychology refutes this claim. One study shows that the jury does not need the standard of objective liability/reasonableness to reach the correct decision.[255] Despite the lack of guidance in the purely subjective liability formula, jurors "get it right by their common sense when there is some substance to the story of the defendant."[256] These results are best understood by another empirical study that suggests that society's calculus of liability is *subjective*, complex, and weightier than the law.[257] Its outcome shows gradations rather than dichotomies.[258]

---

[252] *Compare* Regina v. Smith (Morgan), [2001] 1 AC 146, [2000] 4 All ER 289 (mental condition included into reasonableness standard) *with* People v. Pecora, 107 Ill. App. 2d 283, 246 N.E.2d 865 (1969) (mental condition excluded from reasonableness standard)

[253] H.L.A. HART, PUNISHMENT AND RESPONSIBILITY 76 (1968)

[254] ANDREW ASHWORTH, PRINCIPLES OF CRIMINAL LAW 242 (3d ed., 1999).

[255] *Id.* at 803

[256] *Id.* at 803

[257] Norman J. Finkel & Jennifer L. Groscup, *When Mistake Happen: Commonsense Rules of Culpability*, 3 Psych.Pub.Pol & L. 65,118 (1997).

[258] *Id.*

Furthermore, there is no data to support the claim of the protective function of reasonableness. The jurists who pursue this claim mistakenly assume that reasonableness, or the conduct of a "reasonable person," is known. Rather, it is an elastic concept implemented to address a factual inquiry. If the concept of reasonableness is coherently understood by all individuals, the claim of the protective function of reasonableness will stand. Nevertheless, no court has tried to give a definition of reasonableness.[259] In other words, this objective is a valid and comprehensible one but the means of achieving it is unconvincing, since reasonableness is a legal fiction designed to assess the appropriateness of a conduct in a particular set of circumstances.

In sum, while the objective of setting a standard of conduct manifesting the social moral norms is false, the other objectives of educating the public and protecting individuals from unjustified and unexpected behavior are sound and legitimate. However, the reasonableness standard does not advance these objectives.

V. RULE OF SUBSTANCE VERSUS RULE OF EVIDENCE

A recent English court decision concluded that reasonableness or the reasonable person standard was originally created only to explain the law to the jury.[260] This conclusion undermines the importance of the reasonableness standard and inspires us to investigate what type of legal rule is needed in criminal trials as a substitute for the reasonableness standard, which fails to achieve its objectives.

As a primary issue, we may realize that reasonableness as a rule of substance fails to provide a simple, comprehensible test of liability. For instance, in the Model Penal Code, the defense of duress is available under circumstances in "which a person of reasonable firmness would have been unable to resist."[261] In other words, the defense is unavailable when it is reasonable to expect the defendant not to have committed the crime. The issue of assessing sufficient

---

[259]Regina v. McCarthy, [1954] 2 All ER 262, 265, [1954] 2 Q.B 105, 112 (Lord Goddard C. J.)("No court has ever given, nor do we think ever can give, a definition of what constitutes a reasonable or average man. That must be left to the collective good sense of the jury, and what, no doubt, would govern their opinion would be the nature of the retaliation used by the provoked person.")

[260]*See* Regina v. Smith (Morgan), [2001] 1 AC 146, [2000] 4 All ER 289 (Lord Hoffmann) ("[T]he concept of the "reasonable man" has never been more than a way of explaining the law to a jury; an anthropomorphic image to convey to them, with a suitable degree of vividness, the legal principle that even under provocation, people must conform to an objective standard of behavior which society is entitled to expect"). *See also* Regina v. Dryden [1995] 4 All ER 987, 997 (Lord Taylor) "The purpose of taking the reasonable man was to have a yardstick to measure the loss of self-control that will be permitted to found a defense of provocation."

[261] MODEL PENAL CODE § 2.09(1) (Proposed Official Draft 1962).

control over a state of affairs is very difficult to capture in a simple rule of substance.[262]

Furthermore, a single rule of substance (i.e., test of reasonableness) does not reflect our social expectations. In terms of the reasonableness requirement in the mistake defense, the background emotions of the rapist (lustful, self-seeking), the defender of another (hot headed), and the police officer (calm and restrained) should lead to different cognitive tests.[263] Where emotions are bad, we should expect a higher standard of reasonableness, but where they are good, the test of reasonableness requires their augmentation by the moral judgment of the society.[264]

What we need is a flexible rule that incorporates the two objectives of the reasonableness standard—educating the public and protecting individuals from unjustified, unexpected behavior—and considers the defendant's actual state of mind. To be sure, reasonableness does not consider at all the defendant's actual state of mind. In fact, adopting reasonableness in its purely objective form or in its hybrid subjective/objective form would change the decision matrix from resolving questions of fact to resolving questions of law. Instead of exploring the defendant's actual intent and thereby designing a rule to deal with the individual's behavior in modern society, the objectivity of reasonableness offers a magical device that transforms questions of facts to questions of law by implanting a median standard of reasonableness that reflects the desired standard of conduct. The defendant's liability is not determined according to intent but rather by the social appropriateness of a conduct.[265]

Ignoring the defendant's state of mind raises some fairness considerations. There is a substantial fear that many morally innocent defendants who fall below the standard of reasonableness are unfairly convicted. The courts show no consideration to the defendant's state of mind when

---

[262]*See* Douglas Husak, DOES THE CRIMINAL LIABILITY REQUIRE AN ACT? *in* PHILOSOPHY AND THE CRIMINAL LAW, PRINCIPAL AND CRITIQUE 80-81 (Antony Duff ed., 1998)

[263] Jeremy Horder, *Cognation , Emotion and Criminal Liability* ,L. Q. Rev. 106,469-486(1990)

[264] *Id.*

[265] In discussing the provocation defense, Professor Singer realized the tendency of ignoring the actual mental state of the accused through creating an inflexible rule of law. He observed:

> [A] System which precludes evidence of words which actually enraged the defendant to the point of loss of self control, which precludes evidence of his victim's adultery unless the defendant saw the physical act itself,...and which views the question of cooling off as one of law rather than of fact has, for all practical purposes, relegated the defendant to the sidelines. The issue of his culpability has, thus, been transformed into one to be measured by rules, rather than by his actual mental state

Richard Singer, *The Resurgence of Mens Rea: I-Provocation, Emotional Disturbance, and The Model Penal Code,* 27 B.C.L.Rev.243, 280 (1986)

resolving the question of reasonableness.[266] Consider *Regina v. Ward*.[267] The defendant, a man of "sub-normal" intelligence, was charged with the murder of a small child. The defendant testified that when the child was crying he picked her up and shook her until she stopped. Forensic evidence showed that the child died as a result of the defendant's shaking. However, he did not understand that he was harming her. Neither the defendant's actual mental state nor his partial mental disability was considered in the jury instructions.[268] Consequently, the defendant was convicted of murder. The question arose: does convicting the defendant of murder serve the objectives of reasonableness? The conviction will demoralize society, since the underlying message of such a conviction is that we punish individuals for their stupidity rather than the wrongfulness of their conduct.[269] Punishing the defendant of "sub-normal" intelligence will not protect society from future conduct that is a product of mental disability.[270] Moreover, apart from strict liability offenses, the punishment is warranted only if there is a fault element in the crime.[271] Obviously, fault is lacking because the defendant's

---

[266] *See* State v. Mc Allister, 41 N.J. 342; 196 A.2d 786(1964) (citation omitted)(emphasis added). The case asserted that:

> The provocation which at common law reduces a homicide to manslaughter must be such as is calculated to produce hot blood or passion in a reasonable man, an average man of ordinary self-control. Unless it meets this objective standard of reasonableness, the subjective fact of passion does not make the killing manslaughter. Such *factors as mental abnormality or intoxication are therefore irrelevant*, since the "reasonable man" standard postulates a sane and sober man.

Id.

[267] Regina v. Ward, [1956] 1 Q.B. 351.

[268] The trial judge instructions read, "If, when he did the act which he did do, he must as a reasonable man have contemplated that death or grievous bodily harm was likely to result to the child as a result of what he did, then, members of the jury, if you are satisfied about that, he is guilty of murder", Regina v. Ward, [[1956] 1 Q.B. 351.

[269] Professor Glanville Williams in response to Morgan's decision (D.P.P v. Morgan [1975]2 ALL. E.R 374) stated: "To convict the stupid man [in reference to the unreasonable man] would be to convict him for what lawyers call inadvertent negligence—the honest conduct which may be the best that man can do but that does not come up to the so-called reasonable man" Letter from Glanville Williams, to Times of London (May 8, 1975), *reprinted in* SANFORD H. KADISH & STEPHEN J SCHULHOFER, CRIMINAL LAW AND ITS PROCESS 323 (6th ed. 1994).

[270] The punishment is inefficacious where "the penal provision, thought it was conveyed to the individual notice, could produce no effect with respect to preventing his engaging in the fact prohibited: as in case of extreme infancy, insanity and intoxication" JEREMY BENTHAM, THE RATIONALE OF PUNISHMENT 24 (1830).

[271] *See* A.P. Simester & A.T.H. Smith, CRIMINALIZATION AND THE ROLE OF THEORY, *in* HARM AND CULPABILITY 6 (A.P. Simester & A.T.H. Smith ed., 1996)("Criminalization of harms cannot be accounted for without reference to fault….") *See also* H. L .A. HART, PUNISHMENT AND RESPONSIBILITY 40(1968) ("[I]t is morally permissible to punish only voluntary commission of a moral wrong").

conduct was a product of his mental disability. Therefore, the punishment is unwarranted.

One possible solution to avoid the problem of unfairness is to adopt a purely subjective standard of liability. However, this solution does not serve the objectives of reasonableness, and the standard for judgment would collapse into the personal characteristics of the defendants.[272] It would open the door for lawlessness and disorder by accepting futile allegations of the defendant's special traits. This is the dilemma that was created by adopting a rule of substance to resolve factual questions. By contrast, an evidential rule may offer the flexibility needed for balancing considerations of fairness to a particular defendant and the social policy necessitated by modern society. The jury as representative of the social moral conscience will be able to strike this balance after being informed of our social policy (i.e., the objectives of reasonableness) and the very personal characteristics of a defendant. However, it is also fair to tell the jury that the society assumes that a law-abiding citizen will meet the social expectation under particular circumstances. For instance, we assume that mere insulting words do not justify killing. Nor do we assume that negative feelings of envy, jealously, or greed are sufficient provocation to mitigate homicide. These assumptions are very similar to the legal presumption that all people are sane because the vast majority is sane. These assumptions are not created by legislative bodies; rather, they are embodied in the natural course of actions.[273]

Giving weight to these facts and to numerous courts' decisions suggesting that reasonableness was invented to reflect the social expectation of a conduct,[274] or "social assumptions," the wished-for rule of evidence is self-suggested. It must fall into a recognized legal category of presumptions or inferences. This matter requires further examination.

VI. PRESUMPTIONS AND INFERENCES IN CRIMINAL LAW AS VERIFICATION TO A REASONABLE PERSON STANDARD

There are several alternative theoretical backgrounds for presumptions and inferences in criminal law. Two dominants theories offer persuasive explanations of the "reasonable person" rule as a presumption or permissive inference. The probabilities theory suggests that a presumption can be created

---

[272] GEORGE P. FLETCHER, RETHINKING CRIMINAL LAW 513(1978)

[273] *See* State v. Grilz, 136 Ariz. 450; 666 P.2d 1059 (Ariz. 1983) (Upholding the conclusion that presumption of sanity is common law presumption as opposed to statutory presumption).

[274] *See* Lord Diplock in D.P.P v. Camplin [1978] AC 705, [1978] 2 All ER 168. *See also* Lord Slynn in Regina v. Smith (Morgan), [2001] 1 AC 146, [2000] 4 All ER 289.

upon logical probability.[275] When the existence of a fact is overwhelmingly probable then a presumption is fashioned. For example, the presumption of sanity is based upon the logical probability that the vast majority of individuals are sane.[276] A defendant claiming not to be sane may bear the burden of proving his nonconformity with the general rule. Similarly, society expects law-abiding citizens to act or react in a "certain manner." Mere insulting words do not justify or mitigate killing. Similarly, raising self-defense status does not justify using excessive force. There is always a social limit and expectation of individuals to behave in a "certain manner." These "certain manners" are the reasonable person proper, who exhibits expected and acceptable conduct.

Alternatively, public policy theory suggests that presumption can be created to implement public policy.[277] Obviously, the essence of the "reasonable and ordinary person" rule reflects legitimate social guidelines. Furthermore, a public policy suggests that individuals' behavior ought to meet social expectations.

Remarkably, the relationship between reasonableness and inferences or presumptions has been recognized by courts and legislative bodies alike. In some cases, reasonableness gives rise to the inference of fact,[278] while in others the legislature presumes that individuals act reasonably and, therefore, requires the prosecution to overcome such presumptions.[279]

The second phase of analysis investigates the best category of presumptions that is consistent with constitutional rules of presumptions and

---

[275] CLIFFORD S. FISHMAN, JONES ON EVIDENCE, CIVIL AND CRIMINAL 307 (7th ed., 1993)

[276] Thompson v. Dixon, 987 F. 2d 1038 (4th Cir. 1993) (upholding instructions asserting "[S]anity or soundness of mind is the natural condition of people, therefore every one is presumed sane until the contrary is proven"). *See also* United States v. Hendrix 542 F. 2d 879 (2d Cir. 1976) (emphasizing that "Justification for the 'lingering inference' of sanity is found in the common experience that most men are sane"); People v. Silver, 33 N.Y. 2d 475, 481 (NY.1974) (concluding that the presumption of sanity "being the natural and usual condition of the man kind").

[277] *Id.*

[278] *See, e.g.*, State v. Johnson 119 Wn.2d 167; 829 P.2d 1082 (Wash. 1992) (stating "[I]f a person has information which would lead a reasonable person in the same situation to believe that facts exist which are described by law as being a crime. The jury is permitted but not required to find that he or she acted with knowledge."); United States v. Gallo 543 F. 2d 361,367(D.C. Cir. 1976) (explaining that the comparison to the ordinary person has been imported into many legal definitions of knowledge to make it clear to the jury what level of circumstantial evidence is sufficient for it to conclude that the defendant had actual knowledge); State v. Ship 93 Wn.2d 510; 610 P.2d 1322(Wash. 1980)(elaborating that the comparison creates only an inference; the jury must still find subjective knowledge).

[279] A.R.S. § 13-411 (2001) (C). (A person is presumed to be acting reasonably for the purposes of this section if he is acting to prevent the commission of any of the offenses listed in subsection A of this section.).

inferences as expounded by the United States Supreme Court and that employs the "reasonable person" rule objectives explained above.

The common law recognizes three classes of presumptions/inferences:

A. *Praesumptiones juris et de jure*. These types of presumptions are inferences of facts that cannot be challenged by producing contradictory evidence.[280] They are rules of substances disguised in the form of legal inferences.[281] These sorts of presumptions do not differ significantly from the "reasonable person" rule as presently applied in that the defendant cannot offer evidence disproving his conformity to the hypothetical standard of the conduct of a reasonable person. The United States Supreme Court reintroduced this type of conclusive presumption in *Sandstrom v. Montana*, [282] concluding that it is simply a rule of law. It is irrebuttable and requires the trier of fact to definitively find the presumed fact once the basic facts are established. Therefore, adopting this type of presumption may change only the label of a legal doctrine without affecting its essence or consequences.

B. *Praesumptiones juris sed non de jure*. These types of presumptions are inferences of facts that can be challenged by contradictory evidence.[283] In essence, they offer merely *prima facie* proof of the fact presumed, proof that is rebuttable by contradictory evidence or by a stronger presumption that suggests contrary evidence.[284] This type is modernly termed a "mandatory presumption."[285] It is divided into two types. The first type merely shifts the burden of proof to the defendant.[286] Once the defendant meets his burden, the ultimate burden of proof is on the state. The second type of mandatory presumption entirely shifts the burden of proof to the defendant. Reasonableness as a presumption can be considered the logical parallel to the presumption of sanity. They are both based upon the statistical concept that most people are sane and will do as the reasonable person does. An individual failing to conform to the accepted social rule might bear the burden of proving his exceptionality. The rules of the presumption of sanity can be imported into the presumption of reasonableness. Under the presumption of sanity, the state places the burden of production or a low burden of

---

280 J. W. CECIL TURNER, KENNY'S OUTLINES OF THE CRIMINAL LAW 455 (19th. ed. 1966).
281 *Id.*
282 442 U.S. 510, 99 S. Ct. 2450 (1979)
283 J. W. CECIL TURNER, KENNY'S OUTLINES OF THE CRIMINAL LAW 455-456 (19th. ed. 1966).
284 *Id.*
285 CHARLES TILFORD MCCORMICK, 2 MCCORMICK ON EVIDENCE 490 (John William Strong et. al. eds., 4th ed. 1992); *See also* County court of Ulster County v. Allen 442 U.S. 140 (1979).
286 County of Ulster County v. Allen, 442 U.S. 140, 160 (1979).

persuasion on the defendant to prove his insanity.[287] Once the defendant meets his burden, the presumption of sanity vanishes and the state bears the burden of proof of the defendant's sanity beyond a reasonable doubt.[288]

Similarly, under the proposed presumption of reasonableness, the defendant bears the burden of production or a low burden of persuasion to prove his special trait (i.e., subnormal intelligence) that justifies nonconformity with general norms of conducts. Once the defendant satisfies the burden, the burden of proof is transferred to the state to show that the defendant's special trait either does not exist or does not justify nonconformity with the general norms. Proving the defendant's justificatory special trait involves a two-stage procedure: (1) proving the existence of the special trait; and (2) assessing its affect on the defendant's nonconformity with the general norms of conduct. Such an assessment is a factual inquiry that falls entirely in the jury's domain. Logically, the guidelines of the assessment are the objectives of reasonableness and the defendant's actual state of mind. In this context, we advise the jury that the law presumes that the defendant should have conformed to the general norms of conduct (i.e., acting reasonably in the circumstances as would an ordinary person possessing the *natural* characteristics of the defendant). The jury may reach this factual determination by balancing the state's interest (manifested in advancing the objectives of the presumption of reasonableness as protecting individuals from unjustified, unexpected behavior) and the defendant's interest (manifested in considering his actual state of mind).

It should be noted that incorporating rules of the presumption of sanity

---

[287] There are a number of variations regarding the burden of the defendant; in some jurisdictions, insanity is an affirmative defense that the defendant must prove by the *preponderance of evidence*. *See, e.g.*, L.S.A- C.C.P. art 652; State v. Scott 21 So. 271 (La. 1897); State v. Willie, 360 So. 2d 813 (La. 1978), State v. Watkins, 340 So. 2d 235 (La. 1976); State v. Lee 395 So. 2d 700 (declining to consider the statue unconstitutional relying on Patterson v. New York 432 U.S. 197, 97 S. Ct. 2319, 53 L. Ed.2d. 281(1977)). *See also* Grammer v. State 239 Ala. 633, 196 So. 268 (Ala. 1940) (holding that insanity is an affirmative defense that must be proven by the defendant *to the reasonable satisfaction of the jury*). Some courts require "*some evidence*" to be introduced, which weakens the presumption of sanity. *See, e.g.*, Davis v. United States 160 U.S. 499, 486-487 (1895); Hall v. United States, 295 F.2d 26,27-28(4th Cir. 1961); United States v. Marable, 657 F.2d 75 (4th Cir. 1981); State v. Francis , 233 Kan. 766; 576 P.2d 682 (Kan. 1978). Other courts require the defendant to introduce *"evidence sufficient to present a reasonable doubt of sanity" See e.g.*, Yohn v. State, 476 So. 2d 123(Fla. 1985); Crockham v. State v. 723 So. 2d 355 (Fla. 1998); Young v. State 258 Ind. 246; 280 N.E.2d 595 (Ind.1972) (requiring the defendant in a criminal case to present *"competent or admissible evidence"* on the issue of his or her sanity).

[288] Yohn v. State, 476 So. 2d 123(Fla. 1985) (Once the accused introduces evidence sufficient to present a reasonable doubt of sanity, the presumption of sanity vanishes and the accused's sanity must be proven beyond a reasonable doubt).

into the reasonableness doctrine would likely be held constitutional, given that the presumption of sanity's constitutionality is regularly approved by federal and state courts alike.[289]

Mandatory presumptions *may* violate the Due Process Clause of the Fourteenth Amendment, which prohibits the state from using evidential presumptions in jury instructions that have the effect of relieving the state of its burden of proof beyond a reasonable doubt for every essential element of the crime.[290] Therefore, the "reasonable person" rule cannot be formulated as a mandatory presumption if, and only if, presuming that the defendant should have acted in a particular manner, conforming to the "reasonable person" model, would relieve the state of its burden of proving the elements of the offense.[291]

C. *Praesumptiones hominis* (or *praesumptiones facti*). These are inferences of facts that the law permits but does not compel the jury to draw.[292] The law does not allocate the burden of proof to the defendant with respect to the inferred facts.[293] The United States Supreme Court termed this category "permissive presumption."[294] However, such terminology will only cause jury confusion,[295] since presumptions compel the fact finder to draw a conclusion based upon proving certain

---

[289] *See, e.g.*, Leland v. Oregon, 343 U.S.790, 96 L. Ed. 1302,72 S.Ct.1002(1952)(state may impose burden of proving insanity on the defendant); Medina v. California 120 L. Ed.2d 353, 112 S. Ct. 2572(1992) (a state may establish a presumption that defendant is competent to stand trail and make him shoulder the burden of overcoming the presumption); Stanly v. Mabry , 596 F. 2d 322 (7th Cir), 444 U.S. 946, 62 L. Ed. 2d 315, 100 S. Ct. 307 (1979). Stanly held:

> [W]here jury instructed state had burden to prove beyond reasonable doubt every element of a crime, no constitutional violation occurred by placing burden of proof on defendant to prove his sanity, despite contention that element of malice aforethought in murder charge was so inextricably intertwined with presumption of sanity that to require defendant to prove his insanity required him to disprove an essential element of the offense.

Id.

[290] *In Re* Winship 397 U.S. 358(1970)

[291] *See, e.g.*, Patterson v. New York 432 U.S. 197 (1977); Sandstrom v. Montana ,422 U.S 510(1979) (invalidating instruction stating " the law presumes that a person intended the ordinary consequences of his voluntary acts"); Francis v. Franklin 471U.S.307(1985)

[292] J. W. CECIL TURNER, KENNY'S OUTLINES OF THE CRIMINAL LAW 456(19th. ed. 1966).

[293] CHARLES TILFORD MCCORMICK, 2 MCCORMICK ON EVIDENCE 489 (John William Strong et al. eds., 4th ed. 1992). *See also* County court of Ulster County v. Allen 442 U.S. 140, 157(1979)(A "permissive presumption" allows, but does not require, the fact finder to infer the "element fact" from proof of the basic fact, and places no burden of any kind on the defendant).

[294] County court of Ulster County v. Allen 442 U.S. 140 (1979).

[295] CHARLES TILFORD MCCORMICK, 2 MCCORMICK ON EVIDENCE 450-451(John William Strong et al. eds., 4th ed. 1992).

underlying facts.[296] On the other hand, inferences do not command the fact finder to reach a particular conclusion. The fact finder is free to reject or credit the inference based upon the compelling nature of the facts that underlie the inference.[297] A number of lower courts' decisions demonstrate that advising the jury that it "may infer" the suggested conclusion from basic facts is the preferable formula.[298] Therefore, for the purpose of clarity, this category is better termed "permissive inferences."

Inferences are subject to the rationality requirement of the Due Process Clause, which requires that the fact to be inferred be "more likely than not," giving weight to the facts that underlie the inference.[299] Obviously the use of permissive inferences passes the rationality requirement test because the "reasonable person" hypothetically symbolizes an average, ordinary person. Such a hypothetical person is not more than a representative of the general community's acceptable standard of behavior. The "reasonable person" behaves as do the vast majority of individuals.[300] Therefore, the conduct of the "reasonable person" is "more probable than not," since the vast majority of individuals behave like him.

By implementing permissive inference instructions, we advise the jury to consider the implications of the circumstantial evidence and ensure they may draw conclusions from such evidence.[301] Thus, adopting permissive inference

---

[296] *Id.*

[297] Shari L. Jacobson, *Special Topics in The Law of Evidence: Mandatory and Permissive Presumption in Criminal Cases: The Morass Created by Allen*, 42 U. Miami L.Rev.1009,1010(1988).

[298] United Stats v. Graham, 858 F.2d 986,992(5th Cir. 1988)(approving instruction that jury "may draw the inference" that defendant intended "all the consequences which one standing in like circumstances and possessing like knowledge" would expect), Cert denied, 489 U.S.1020;United States v. Silvia , 745 F.2d 840,851-852 (4th Cir.1984)(upholding instruction that "[I]t is reasonable to infer that a person ordinarily intends the natural and probable consequences of acts...")cert.denied,470 U.S.1031; United States v. Vreeken, 803 F.2d 1085,1092(10th Cir.1986)(upholding instruction that "[y]ou may consider it reasonable to draw the inference and find that a person intends the natural and the probable consequences of acts knowingly done" Cert denied ,484 U.S. 963.

[299] County court of Ulster County v. Allen 442 U.S. 140, 165-167(1979). *See also* Leary v. United States, 395 U.S.6, 36-39 (1969)(presumption that person possessing marijuana knows it is imported is irrational and arbitrary); Tot v. United States, 319 U.S.463, 467(1943) (invalidating presumption that possession of firearm was presumptive evidence that the weapon was received in interstate commerce).

[300] *See* Masciantonio v. Regina. (1995) 183 C.L.R 58; Paul H Robinson, *A Theory of Justification: Societal Harm as Prerequisite To Criminal Liability*, 23 U.C.L A. L Rev. 266(1975)

[301] CHRISTOPHER B. MUELLER & LAIRD C. KIRKPATRICK, MODERN EVIDENCE: DOCTRINE AND PRACTICE 236 (1995).

analysis as an explanation for the "reasonable person" serves the objectives of the "reasonable person" rule. We enforce the public policy of protecting individuals from unjustified, unexpected behavior by making an inference that the defendant should have acted in a particular manner conforming to the behavior of an average person who possesses the personal characteristics of the defendant (i.e., age, intelligence level, gender, cultural and ethnic background). We educate the jury regarding the public policy by pronouncing the societal values and policy considerations underlying the inference. Moreover, we advise the jury to consider the defendant's actual state of mind. By doing so, we ensure paramount consideration of the objectives of the "reasonable person" rule, but we also give the innocent defendant a window of opportunity to rebut the inference with evidence examined at trial. Any unusual characteristics of the defendant may be presented and proved. In this context, the jury strikes a balance between public policy considerations and fairness considerations manifested in considering the defendant's actual state of mind.

VII. CONCLUSION

The doctrine of reasonableness is not in and of itself a bad one, but framing it as a rule of substance diverts our attention from the true nature of reasonableness as a factual inquiry, which should be assessed by evidentiary rule. Reasonableness is troubled by the circular competing considerations of objective and subjective liability. As a rule of substance it fails to achieve its objectives and ignores the defendant's state of mind. By contrast, reasonableness as a rule of evidence can advance the stated objectives and gives realistic weight to the defendant's actual state of mind.

Reasonableness as a rule of evidence is best framed as a mandatory presumption or permissive inference. It depends on evaluating the priorities at stake. Those priorities are the state's interests in protecting individuals from unjustified, unexpected behavior, and the defendant's interests, which require a consideration of his actual state of mind. Legislative bodies and courts may adopt either evidentiary rule. In the selection process, the courts and the legislatures must consider the most distinguishing feature of inferences to be that they remain in the case despite the presentation of contrary proof. Unlike presumptions, which do not survive, the production of competent evidence may tend to prove the contrary of the presumed fact.[302] Reasonableness as an inference gives the jury broad power in assessing the reasonableness of a conduct. In contrast, reasonableness as a presumption restricts jury assessment by placing the burden of proof on the defendant or distributing it between the defendant and the state. So long as criminal law is our concern, it is preferable to adopt the permissive inference rule because the risk of erroneous conviction greatly outweighs the state's interest.

---

[302] Thompson v. State 646 N.E. 2d 687 (Ind. 1995).

VIII. PROPOSED JURY INSTRUCTIONS

A. REASONABLENESS AS PERMISSIVE INFERENCE

You have heard the reasonableness or "reasonable person/reasonable man" requirement. This requirement allows you to infer that the defendant should have acted as an average, ordinary person would—specifically, as one who possesses the defendant's particular characteristics, such as age, gender, intelligence level, educational and cultural background, and any other characteristics that distinguish the defendant from the general community. However, you should know that you are free to draw or ignore the inference. This requirement was design to protect individuals from unjustified, unexpected risks. The defendant has the right to rebut this inference through the introduction of evidence. If you believe that there is sufficient evidence to rebut the inference, do not hold the defendant accountable as a reasonable person. If the inference is rebutted by sufficient evidence, you must hold the defendant liable according to what he actually believed.

B. REASONABLENESS AS MANDATORY PRESUMPTION

1. Type One, Which Merely Shifts the Burden of Production to the Defendant

You have heard the reasonableness or "reasonable person/reasonable man" requirement. This requirement presumes that the defendant should have acted as an average, ordinary person would—specifically, as one who possesses the defendant's particular characteristics, such as age, gender, intelligence level, educational and cultural background, and any other characteristics that distinguish the defendant from the general community. This requirement was designed to protect individuals from unjustified, unexpected risks. In your assessment as to the reasonableness of the defendant's conduct, you must consider the defendant's actual state of mind. You must hold the defendant accountable as a reasonable person, unless the defendant offers satisfactory evidence sufficient to rebut this presumption. Once the defendant offers such evidence, the state must disprove the evidence presented by the defendant (beyond a reasonable doubt, if reasonableness is integrated into the elements of the offense; otherwise, to the satisfaction of the jury). If the state fails to disprove the defendant's evidence, you must hold the defendant accountable according to what he actually believed.

2. Type Two, Which Shifts the Ultimate Burden of Proof to the Defendant

You have heard the reasonableness or "reasonable person/reasonable man" requirement. This requirement presumes that the defendant should have acted as an average, ordinary person would—specifically, as one who possesses the defendant's characteristics, such as age, gender, intelligence level, educational and cultural background, and any other characteristics that distinguish the defendant from the general community. This requirement was designed to protect individuals from unjustified, unexpected risks. In your assessment as to the reasonableness of the defendant's conduct, you must consider the defendant's actual state of mind. You must hold the defendant accountable as a reasonable person unless the defendant has offered satisfactory evidence sufficient to rebut this presumption.

It should be noted that this type of mandatory presumption is unconstitutional if reasonableness is an element of the offense or integrated into an element of the offense, because it relieves the state of its burden of proving the elements of the offense.[303]

---

[303] *See, e.g.*, Patterson v. New York 432 U.S. 197 (1977); Sandstrom v. Montana ,422 U.S 510(1979); Francis v. Franklin 471U.S.307(1985).

Chapter Three

Recklessness

I. INTRODUCTION

Mens rea of homicide offense can be divided into three main categories: cognitive state of belief (i.e., knowing that particular conduct will cause certain results), the state of desire (i.e., purposeful killing), and the mental state that lacks both belief and desire, normally articulated as negligence.

This classification of the mental elements of homicide was originally created by the common law and reformulated in the Model Penal Code. The Model Penal Code describes four mental states: purposely, knowingly, recklessly, and negligently.[304] The mental states of murder consist of two cognitive states of belief: knowingly and recklessness indifference to human life and one a state of desire, namely purposely.[305] A lesser degree of recklessness qualifies for manslaughter.[306] If the actor lacked the state of desire and the cognitive state of belief, then he is liable for the lesser offense of negligent homicide.[307] The only exception to the desire/belief classification is the addition of the provocation defense to the definition of manslaughter, under the label of extreme mental or emotional disturbance.[308] The Model Penal Code culpability scheme almost mirrors that of the common law. Malice aforethought, which is required for murder includes the state of desire[309]—or "purposely," as the Model Penal Code defines it—the cognitive state of belief of knowledge of the

[304] MODEL PENAL CODE § 2.02(2) (Proposed Official Draft 1962).
[305] *Id.* § 2.10.2(1).
[306] *Id.* § 2.10.3(1) (a).
[307] *Id.* § 2.10.4(1).
[308] *Id.* § 2.10.3(1) (b).
[309] ("Express Malice is when one, with a sedate deliberate mind and formed design, doth kill another")WILLIAM BLACKSTONE, 4 COMMENTARIES ON THE LAWS OF ENGLAND 199(1st. ed 1769)

consequences and the cognitive state of belief of reckless indifference.[310] The mental state of manslaughter under the common law is satisfied by a reckless killing or a desired killing committed under provocation.[311] The only significant difference between the Model Penal Code and common law is that the former created a new crime category, negligent homicide, which ordinarily under the common law is included within either misfortune killing or manslaughter, as the case may be.[312]

Since the Model Penal Code reflects the proper understanding of common law, my analysis will follow its scheme. This chapter will discuss the cognitive state of belief of recklessness while focusing on the core concept of all cognitive states of belief, namely knowledge. Knowledge is important in defining not only the cognitive states of belief, such as knowingly or recklessly, but also the (negative) mental state of negligent, by showing that a defendant lacked both the cognitive state of belief and the state of desire.

II. PROBLEMS WITH SETTING RECKLESSNESS BOUNDARIES

Recklessness is probably the most important culpability standard under the Model Penal Code because it is the default mental state. It is the *presumed* mental state when a criminal statute is silent regarding the required culpable mental state in a specific offense.[313] Despite its importance, it encounters several

---

[310] ("Neither shall he be guilty of less crime [than murder], who kills another in consequence of such a willful act, as shews him to be enemy to all mankind in general; as going deliberately with a horse used to strike, or discharging a gun, among a multitude of people…and, if two or more come together to do an unlawful act against the king's peace, of which the probable consequence might be bloodshed; as to beat a man, to commit riot, or rob a park; and one of them kills a man; it is murder in them all, because of the unlawful act, the *militia praecogitata*, or evil intended beforehand.") *Id.* at 200.

[311] ("Manslaughter is therefore thus defined, the unlawful killing of another, without malice either express or implied: which either voluntarily, upon sudden heat; or involuntarily, but in the commission of some unlawful act.") *Id.* at 191. Involuntary homicide committed by unlawful act corresponds to the modern terminology of reckless homicide. *See* ("so where a person does an act, lawful in itself, but in unlawful manner, and without due caution and circumscription: as when a workman flings down a stone or piece of timber into the street, and kills a man; this may be either misadventure, manslaughter or murder according to the circumstances under which the original act was done…if it were in London, or other populous town, where people are continually passing it is manslaughter, though he gives loud warning; and murder if he knows of their passing and gives no warning at all, for then it is malice against all mankind.") *Id.* at 192

[312] ("In the case of misadventure, it presumes negligence, or at least a want of sufficient caution in him who was so unfortunate as to commit it; who therefore is not altogether faultless.") *Id.* at 186.

[313] (Culpability Required Unless Otherwise Provided. When the culpability sufficient to establish a material element of an offense is not prescribed by law, such element is

definitional and practical problems. The definitional problems are closely associated with a unique feature in the Model Penal Code's culpability scheme involving fine distinctions in the degree and type of knowledge. In "purposely," the actor is aware of the risk of harm.[314] In "knowingly," the actor is aware of the high probability that harm would occur.[315] In "recklessly," there is a substantial risk of harm.[316] In "negligently," the actor is unaware of the risk of harm; however he should have been aware of it.[317] The hair-splitting distinction between "knowledge of the substantial risk of harm" and "knowledge of the high probability of the risk of harm" is difficult to comprehend. So as far as criminal homicide is concerned, the Model Penal Code offers a partial solution by suggesting that a high degree of recklessness that shows indifference to the value of human life qualifies for murder.[318] On the other hand, less extreme recklessness should be treated as manslaughter.[319] Therefore, the confusion generated as a result of definitional similarities will have no practical effect with respect to murder. However, the problem remains with regard to manslaughter in which the distinction between knowledge of *substantial risk of harm* and knowledge of the *high probability of the risk of harm* determines liability. If a jury cannot properly distinguish between the degrees of knowledge of harm but is given the choice of convicting for manslaughter or murder, the conviction for either offense will be arbitrary.

The Model Penal Code neither offers nor is able to offer a clear distinction under its present culpability scheme. The only visible solution is to

---

established if a person acts purposely, knowingly or recklessly with respect thereto) MODEL PENAL CODE § 2.02(3) (Proposed Official Draft 1962).

[314] MODEL PENAL CODE § 2.02(2) (a) (Proposed Official Draft 1962). *See also* 1 SUBSTANTIVE CRIMINAL LAW, WAYNE R. LA FAVE & AUSTIN W. SCOTT 336(1986).

[315] MODEL PENAL CODE § 2.02(2) (b) (Proposed Official Draft 1962).

[316] MODEL PENAL CODE § 2.02(2) (c) (Proposed Official Draft 1962). The Model Penal Code adopts the subjective liability scheme that the actor should be actually aware of the risk. *See* Ira P. Robins, *Criminal Law: The Ostrich Instruction: Deliberate Ignorance as A Criminal Mens Rea,* 81 J. Crim. L. & Criminology 191,222-223(1990). *Compare* the traditional common approach, which relies upon the objective liability concept of reasonableness. *See* GLANVILLE WILLIAMS, TEXT BOOK OF CRIMINAL LAW 96 (2d ed .1983). Professor Williams states: "recklessness ([N]ormally involves conscious and *unreasonable* risk-taking either as to the possibility that a particular undesirable circumstances exists or to the possibility that some evil will come to pass) *Id.*

[317] MODEL PENAL CODE § 2.02(2) (d) (Proposed Official Draft 1962).

[318] The Model Penal Code drafters observed:

> It must be left directly to the trier of fact under instructions which make it clear that recklessness that can fairly be assimilated to purpose or knowledge should be treated as murder and that less extreme recklessness should be treated as manslaughter.

2 MODEL PENAL CODE AND COMMENTARIES 22 (Official Draft and Revised Comment 1980).

[319] *Id.*

redefine either "recklessness" or "knowingly." This is a matter exclusively within the legislature's power, and, therefore, far beyond the scope of this book.

The practical problem is that the Code is silent as to whether reckless homicide is the lesser offense, which is encompasses reckless indifference, leaving it to the courts' conflicting opinions.[320]

On the other hand, the states that continue to follow the common law culpability scheme struggle with the definition of "reckless homicide."[321] Some courts have held that depraved-heart murder, which is a form of reckless homicide, and negligent homicide are distinguishable simply by the degree of recklessness.[322] They concede that depraved-heart murder involves a higher degree of recklessness than negligent homicide.[323] Others erode the distinction between recklessness and negligence by emphasizing that criminal negligence must involve reckless indifference to the value of the human life.[324]

Some jurisdictions, such as New Mexico, rely upon the objective/subjective liability distinction to differentiate between first- and

---

[320] *See, e.g.*, Lyttle v. State, 709 N.E.2d 1, 5(Ind.1999) (Reckless homicide is inherently included in murder); State v. Kramar, 440 N.W.2d 317, 327 (Wis.1989) (A jury is to be given a lesser-included instruction only when there are reasonable grounds in the evidence both for acquittal on the greater charge and conviction on the lesser offense); State v. Gourdine, 472 S.E.2d 241,242 (S.C .1996) (The trial judge is to charge the jury on a lesser included offense if there is any evidence from which the jury could infer that the lesser, rather than the greater, offense was committed.).

[321] Interestingly enough that lack of clarity in reckless homicide is an everlasting problem. Professor Remington more than fifty years ago criticized the unprincipled methodologies of defining reckless conduct. He maintained that states used various confusing terminologies to describe the same mental state. *See* Frank Remington & Orrin L. Helstad, *The Mental Element In Crime-A Legislative Problem*, 1952 Wis. L. Rev 644,664.

[322] Windham v. State, 602 So.2d 798,801(Miss.1992); *See also* Jones v. State, 710 So.2d 870,878(Miss.1998) (Malice too may be inferred when such a high degree of recklessness is involved, raising the level of the crime from "culpable negligence" manslaughter to depraved heart murder).

[323] *Windham*, 602 So.2d at 80; *Jones*, 710 So.2d at 878.

[324] State v. Weiner, 194 A. 2d 467, 470 (N.J.1963) (Negligence, to be criminal, must be reckless and wanton and of such character as shows an utter disregard for the safety of others under circumstances likely to cause death); Cain v. State, 190 S.E. 371,375(GA.1937) (The violation of the safety statute regulating the use of highways does not constitute criminal negligence, unless such violation is intentional, willful, or wanton, or unless the violation, though unintentional, is accompanied by recklessness or is under circumstances from which probable death or injury to others might be reasonably anticipated.); Geele v. State, 47 S.E.2d 283,287(GA.1948) (The court emphasized that negligence, carelessness, and recklessness under the involuntary-manslaughter statute to mean the same thing), *followed in* Payne v. State, 394 S.E.2d 781,783(GA.1990). *See also* Robinson v. Commonwealth, 569 S.W.2d 183(ky.Ct.App.1978) (defining reckless homicide as "failure to perceive a substantial and unjustified risk when such failure is a gross deviation from standard of care that a reasonable person would observe in the situation").

second-degree homicide. The New Mexico courts held that reckless homicide can be either first- or second-degree murder; however, subjective knowledge of risk is required in first-degree murder while second-degree homicide requires only objective knowledge of risk.[325] To make matters worse, the New Mexico courts give subjective knowledge an objective standard of liability definition. The courts held that "subjective knowledge exists if the defendants' conduct was very risky, and under the circumstances known to the defendants that they *should have realized* this very high degree of risk."[326]

The recklessness liability scheme in the jurisdictions that continue to follow the common law is, indeed, problematic. In the New Mexico culpability grading system, the subjective/objective distinction is useful only for inferring the requisite mental state rather than for setting the standard for liability. In other words, under the subjective liability standard, the jury adopts the defendant's point of view with regard to the defendant's awareness of risk. Under the objective liability standard, the jury inquires whether a reasonable person in the defendant's position would have been aware of the risk. In both cases, the jury is free to infer the existence of awareness of the risk from the defendant's testimony, the circumstances, and the evidence in general. Therefore, the subjective/objective scheme is *a guiding evidential rule* rather than determinative of the level of culpability.

In general, the jurisprudence of recklessness in New Mexico—along with other jurisdictions that distinguish between recklessness and negligence by the degree of recklessness,[327] or equate recklessness with negligence[328]—faces a number of challenges.

First, the hierarchy of culpability, intentionality and quasi-intentionality (purpose, knowledge), recklessness, and negligence becomes confused and indistinct.[329] The contention that negligence involves a lesser degree of recklessness, or that negligence is recklessness, and the inappropriate use of

---

[325] State v. Brown, 931 P. 2d 69, 72-73(N.M. 1996). *See also* People v. Watson, 637 P.2d 279,283(Cal.1981) (The court relied upon objective/subjective liability distinction to distinguish between implied malice required for first-degree murder and gross negligence require for vehicular manslaughter).

[326] *See* State v. McCrary, 675 P.2d 120,122(N.M.1984) (The court emphasized that "the jury decides whether there is a subjective knowledge of risk by considering 'what the defendant should realize' to be the degree of risk, in the light of the surrounding circumstances which he knows") *Id.*

[327] Windham v. State, 602 So.2d 798,801(Miss.1992); Jones v. State, 710 So.2d 870,878(Miss.1998).

[328] State v. Weiner, 194 A. 2d 467, 470 (N.J.1963); Geele v. State, 47 S.E.2d 283,287(GA.1948). State v. Clark, 446 So. 2d 293,298(La.1984) (holding that the term "criminal negligence" means gross negligence or recklessness such as to amount to a reckless disregard for one's own safety or the safety of others and a willful indifference to the consequences liable to follow).

[329] *See* RICHARD SINGER & JOHN LA FOND, CRIMINAL LAW 45-53 (1997). *See also* MODEL PENAL CODE § 2.02 (Proposed Official Draft 1962). *See also* United States v. Bailey 444 U.S. 394, 404(1980).

evidential rules of subjective/objective distinction to determine levels of culpability disrupt the hierarchy of culpability.

Differentiating levels of culpability based on the degree of recklessness is a suitable and common practice in the states that follow the Model Penal Code. It is typically stated that the actor who is practically certain of causing harm is more culpable than the one who takes substantial risk of causing harm.[330] However, it is inconceivable to say that negligence involves a lesser degree of recklessness or that negligence is recklessness. To say that is to defy the natural meaning of the term "negligence." It would confuse the jury, since negligence would then become legal jargon that needs a new and comprehensive definition. Therefore, the problem is not limited to the confusing hierarchy of culpability, with the labeling of negligence as a lesser degree of recklessness or as utter recklessness, but also includes the odd usage of the English language, which then opens the door for further confusion.

When the New Mexico recklessness grading scheme makes a distinction between two degrees of homicide simply by invoking the subjective/objective liability distinction, it differentiates between two distinctive degrees of moral culpability by the method of inferring culpability. In essence, this grading scheme unjustifiably equates two degrees of moral culpability.

Second, codifying two degrees of homicide that have no material difference in their mental elements, as is seen in the New Mexico recklessness grading scheme, may create a constitutional problem.

The United States Supreme Court acknowledged the government's broad discretionary power in selection of the charges to be brought in a particular case.[331] Moreover, the Court held that a criminal statute that prescribes different degrees of punishment for the same conduct does not violate a person's right to equal protection of the law unless the prohibited conduct or the authorized punishment is not clearly defined.[332] It follows, then, that when two criminal statutes, such as reckless and negligent homicide, or two indistinguishable degrees of reckless homicide, prescribe different penalties for the same conduct, the government may select either or both statutes as its basis for prosecution. However, these criminal statutes are invalid if they "fail to give a person of ordinary intelligence fair notice that his contemplated conduct is forbidden."[333]

Applying the jurisprudence established in these Supreme Court decisions, we may conclude that the New Mexico recklessness grading scheme and similar statutes are likely to be held unconstitutional, not for violation of Equal Protection of Laws, but rather for the vagueness of the conduct prohibited. The vagueness stems from utilizing a subjective/objective liability distinction, which is in fact an evidential rule, to distinguish between two morally distinct

---

[330] *See* MODEL PENAL CODE § 2.02(2) (b) &(c) (Proposed Official Draft 1962).
[331] United States v. Goodwin, 457 U.S.368, 382 (1982).
[332] United States v. Batchelder, 442 U.S. 114, 23(1979).
[333] United States v. Harriss, 347 U.S. 612, 617 (1954).

culpable conducts. It is also stems from giving a subjective standard of liability an objective standard definition,[334] which in turn equates two degrees of homicide, in contradiction to the legislative intent manifested in enacting two degrees of homicide.

In other words, while the legislature clearly intended to create two degrees of homicide and, therefore, prescribe different punishments, this intention is defeated either because the distinction of subjective/objective liability fails to achieve its goal of distinguishing between two offenses, since it is a rule of evidence rather than a rule of substances, or because the New Mexico Supreme Court defined a subjective liability standard in objective terms. Once the legislative distinction between two offenses fails, one would speculate as to the meaning of the two offenses, rendering the offenses vague and unconstitutional.[335]

Yet, there is a judicial tendency to overshadow the negligent mental state by defining it in terms fairly identical to recklessness.[336] Perhaps these courts are driven by a desire to abolish negligence as a basis for criminal liability. Nevertheless, it would better for these courts, instead of creating a constitutional problem, to comment on the morality of punishing negligent persons in order to encourage the legislature to intervene and revise the law.

In sum, although the jurisdictions that I have discussed above represent only a few definitional problems of recklessness, we may conclude the following. Although the Model Penal Code offers some guidance as to the culpable mental states, its analysis falls short of offering a practical distinction between reckless homicide and "knowingly" homicide, which in turn renders many judgments unconstitutional because of the vagueness of the conduct prohibited.[337] Furthermore, the code fails to address the issue of the lesser included offenses with respect to the degree of recklessness. In contrast, the states that continue to follow Common Law struggle with the definition of "recklessness," encountering doctrinal and constitutional problems.

III. OUTLINING RECKLESSNESS BOUNDARIES

Isolating the elements of recklessness depends on whether a state follows the Model Penal Code or continues to follow the common law. The Model Penal Code defines "recklessness" as a conscious disregard of a substantial and unjustified risk.[338] To satisfy this definition, the actor must be *conscious* (which

---

[334] State v. McCrary, 675 P.2d 120,122(N.M.1984).
[335] *See* Lanzetta v. New Jersey, 306 U.S. 451, 453 (1939) (affirming that it is a fundamental tenet of Due Process that "[no] one may be required at peril of life, liberty or property to speculate as to the meaning of penal statutes.")
[336] Geele v. State, 47 S.E.2d 283,287(GA.1948); Robinson v. Commonwealth, 569 S.W.2d 183(ky.Ct.App.1978).
[337] *See* S*upra note* 335 and the accompanying text.
[338] *See* MODEL PENAL CODE § 2.02(2) (c) (Proposed Official Draft 1962).

denotes awareness) of the conduct and the possible consequences of risk taking.[339] The Model Penal Code also requires that the conduct be substantial and unjustified. To be aware that a conduct is substantial, the actor must be aware of the attending circumstances. Similarly, awareness that a conduct is unjustified involves awareness of law. In sum, the actor must be aware of his conduct, the attending circumstances, the law, and the consequences.

From a practical standpoint, it is impossible to define recklessness in the states that continue to follow the common law because of the discrepancy and elusiveness of the concept of recklessness in their jurisdictions.[340] Therefore, the following analysis of recklessness will adopt the Model Penal Code scheme. Nevertheless, this analysis is also a useful guide for states that continue to follow the common law.

A. NATURE OF THE RISK: SUBJECTIVE VERSUS OBJECTIVE AWARENESS

The Model Penal Code recklessness liability formula requires a subjective awareness of risk and an objective deviation from the standard of care, or nonconformity of the conduct to social norms.[341] This formula was strictly adopted in some states,[342] while other states modified it by holding that the actor's subjective knowledge of the risk is irrelevant.[343] As a result, both the awareness of the risk and the deviation from the standard of care were construed objectively.[344]

The courts assessed knowledge of the risk objectively because the lack of direct evidence of knowledge (such as the defendant's admission of awareness of risk),[345] or the requirement of actual knowledge, would predictably constitute a heavy burden for the prosecution, which could not be easily

---

[339] *Id. See also* Joshua Dressler, *The Morality of The Criminal Law: A Symposium in Honor of Professor Sandy Kadish. Does One Mens Rea Fit All?: Thoughts on Alexander Unified Conception of Criminal Culpability*, 88 Calif.L.Rev.955, 959(2000).

[340] *See* Parker v. State, 507 S.E.2d 744,748(GA.1998) (holding that life-endangering acts of recklessness can constitute the implied malice sufficient to authorize a conviction for malice murder.). *See also* State v. Clark, 446 So. 2d 293,298(1984) (concluding that the term "criminal negligence" means gross negligence or recklessness such as to amount to a reckless disregard for one's own safety or the safety of others and a willful indifference to the consequences liable to follow).

[341] *See* MODEL PENAL CODE § 2.02(2) (c) (Proposed Official Draft 1962).

[342] *See* State v. Blair, 437 N.W.2d 566,560(Wis.1991); State v. Edmunds, 598 N.W.2d 290,290(Wis.1999).

[343] People v. Register, 60 N.Y.2d 270,277(N.Y.1983); People v. Davis, 526 N.E.2d 20 (N.Y.1988); Minor v. State,85 Md.App.305, 583 A.2d 1102 (Md.1991).

[344] *Register*,60 N.Y.2d at 277; *Davis*, 526 N.E.2d 20; *Minor*,85 Md.App.305.

[345] *See* State v. Burrow 653 P.2d 226,234(Ore.1982) (holding that "it seldom happens that direct evidence can be produced that the accused had actual knowledge of a fact. And in absence of direct evidence knowledge can be inferred from circumstances").

satisfied[346] or would impair effective enforcement of law.[347] These rationalizations have been consistently rejected by some courts because knowledge can be inferred from the circumstantial evidence.[348]

Neither the subjective nor the objective standard of liability affects the jury's inference of the awareness of the risk.[349] The jurors are not mind readers. They can infer awareness of the risk from the circumstances,[350] the defendant's testimony, or any evidence presented.[351]

Furthermore, there are two potential problems with the jury's objective assessment of knowledge of risk. First, the jury may exclude the personal characteristics of the defendant that may distinguish him from the general community. For instance, in *Regina v. Stone,* [352] the defendant was described as "low average intelligence, partially deaf, almost totally blind and with no appreciable sense of smell."[353] The codefendant, Dobinson, was described as "ineffectual and somewhat inadequate."[354] The jury instructions allowed a conviction upon the failure to perceive a risk rather than actual awareness of risk of death.[355] An average, a reasonable person would, in fact, perceive the risk of death, but these defendants were not average persons. They failed to perceive the risk because of their own inadequacies.[356]

---

346 Abbot C.J in R v. Marsh, (1824) 2 B.& C.717,721

347 *In re* Jorge M., 23 Cal.4th 866,884(2000).

348 Staples v. United States 511 U.S. 600,616-617(1994) (Thomas J.); State v. Burrow 293 Ore.691, 705-706, 653 P.2d 226,234; State v. Pickus, 257 N.W. 284,297(S.D.1934).

349 *See* James Gobert, *Searching For Coherence In The Law of Involuntary Manslaughter: The English Experience*, 6 Crim L.F.435, 452(1995).

350 Staples v. United States 511 U.S. 600,616-617(1994) (Thomas J.). State v. Burrow 653 P.2d 226,234(Ore.1982) (holding that "it seldom happens that direct evidence can be produced that the accused had actual knowledge of a fact. And in absence of direct evidence knowledge can be inferred from circumstances"). Waterman v. State, 40 S.E. 262,264(GA.1901) (Concluding that knowledge can be proved by circumstances, including the opportunities which the accused had to ascertain the facts) *followed in* State v. Pickus, 257 N.W. 284,297(S.D.1934). United States Postal Service Bd. of Governors v. Aikens, 460 U.S. 711, 716-717 (1983) quoting Edgington v. Fitzmaurice, 29 Ch. Div. 459, 483 (1885) (Holding that "the state of a man's mind is as much a fact as the state of his digestion. It is true that it is very difficult to prove what the state of a man's mind at a particular time is, but if it can be ascertained it is as much a fact as anything else....").

351 United States v. Sheiner, 410 F.2d 337,340(2d Cir.1969) quoting Anderson v. United States 270 F.2d 124, 127 (6th Cir.1959), Cert. Denied, 396 U.S.825 (1969) (concluding that knowledge "may be inferred or gathered from the outward manifestations, by the words or acts" of the defendant)

352 Regina v. Stone [1977] 2 All E.R. 341.

353 *Id.*

354 *Id.*

355 *Id.* at 346.

356 *See* James Gobert, *Searching For Coherence in The Law of Involuntary Manslaughter: The English Experience*, 6 Crim L.F.435, 452-453(1995); *Compare* Regina v. Stephenson, (1979) 2 All E.R. 1198 (Crim. App.) (The court reversed an arson

Since the defendant's awareness of the risk can be inferred from any set of circumstances, the fact finder should not be restricted by an objective standard of liability.[357] Factors such as race, gender, age, and culture shape the defendant's moral culpability and therefore should be assessed by the jury.[358] In this context, reasonableness of foreseeing the risk or objective knowledge of risk can be properly construed as a guiding evidential rule. It can be construed as a presumption or inference portraying to the jury the average person's knowledge of risk.[359] However, the jury is free to consider any special traits that may distinguish the defendant from the general community. Alternatively, to convict a person because he did not perceive the risk, due to personal characteristics that do not conform to an objective standard, is to convict him not for his guilt but rather for his disability.[360]

Second, jury instruction *might* be unconstitutional when it creates a mandatory presumption of knowledge if knowledge is an element of the offense.[361] In *State v. Ford*,[362] the court held that "the offender is taken to know that which any reasonable person so situated would have known."[363] However, the court never requested proving what a reasonable person would have known. Thus, the instruction relieves the state from the burden of proving knowledge that is an essential element of the offense.

According to *Winship* guidelines,[364] every state is required to prove the elements of the offense. The states that adopted subjective knowledge of risk as an element of reckless conduct are required to prove such knowledge. Similarly, the states that adopted objective knowledge of risk are also required to prove objective knowledge of risk. In reality, the states that adopted subjective

---

conviction because the trial court failed to instruct the jury properly on the defendant's schizophrenia issue).

357 Larry Alexander, *The Morality of The Criminal Law: A Symposium In Honor of Professor Sandy Kadish: Insufficient Concern: A Unified Conception of Criminal Liability*, 88 Calif.L.Rev.931, 936(2000) (Professor Alexander concluded that "risk is an essentially epistemic concept. Risk is always relative to someone's prospective, a prospective that is defined by possession of certain information but not other information.").

358 *See* Michael H. Hoffheimer, *Murder and Manslaughter In Mississippi: Unintentional Killings*, 71 Miss.L.J.35, 104(2001).

359 United States v. Werner, 160 F.2d 438,441-442(2d Cir.1947) (The court reject the reasonable man rule, holding that the rule may only raise the inference of actual knowledge.)

360 Kasle v. United States, 233 F. 878,887 (6th Cir.1916) (The court criticized the "reasonable person" rule in jury charge rule, holding: "the result of the rule of the charge would be to convict a man, not because guilty, but because stupid").

361 *See* Mullaney v. Wilbur, 421 U.S. 684 (1975).

362 State v. Ford, 473 So. 2d 931(La. Ct. App. 3d Cir.)

363 *Id.* at 934

364 The guidelines are best explained in following three judgments, *In Re* Winship, 397 U.S. 358 (1970), Mullaney v. Wilbur, 421 U.S. 684 (1975), Patterson v. New York, 432 U.S. 197 (1977).

knowledge do offer evidence to prove that the actor actually knows the risk of harm. In contrast, the states that adopted objective knowledge of risk offer no evidence of what a reasonable person would know, thereby relieving themselves from proving an essential element of the offense, contrary to *Winship* directions. Therefore, the objective knowledge approach is unconstitutional if the United States Supreme Court decisively upholds the principles established in *Winship.*[365]

B. THE NECESSITY OF KNOWLEDGE IN CRIMINAL LAW

Two arguments require knowledge as the *source* of culpability. The first argument questions the justifiability of punishment in the absence of knowledge. The second investigates the constitutional necessity of knowledge.

The first argument suggests that to punish an actor justly, the punishment must fulfill one or more of the six punishment rationales.

Under the deterrence theory, punitive sanction is imposed to deter the commission of future crimes, either by discouraging the potential offenders from committing crimes through the threat of the punishment or by discouraging the convicted criminals from reoffending by punishing them for crimes already committed.[366] Whether the targeted agent is a potential offender or a convicted criminal, he can be deterred from committing future crimes *only* if he is aware of his actions, including their consequences, the circumstances, and the criminal sanction imposed for his potential crimes.

The incapacitation rationale suggests that some punitive sanctions, such as imprisonment or the death penalty, restrain the offenders' ability to reoffend.[367] Consequently, restraining the offenders, or "incapacitating" them, will reduce the number of crimes considerably.[368] This rationale suggests that individuals who challenge the social moral code manifest an unwillingness to obey that code in the future. Therefore, society should prevent them from causing further harm in the future by incapacitating them. An agent who is

---

365 397 U.S. 358 (1970).

366 *See* JEREMY BENTHAM, RATIONALE OF PUNISHMENT 19-21(1830). *See also* GEORGE P. FLETCHER, RETHINKING CRIMINAL LAW 414(1978). Jeremy Bentham represents the classical school of deterrence; for modern analysis that incorporates the moral influence on individuals into the deterrence rationale *see* Johannes Andeans, *The General Preventive Effects of punishment*, 114 U. Pa. L. Rev. 949,955(1966). For criticism of deterrence theory *see* Gerald Gardiner, *The Purpose of Criminal Punishment*, 21 Modern L. Rev. 117,121-122(1958) (contending that deterrence rationale fails for two reasons, namely, people continue to commit offenses despite inflicting the punitive sanction on offenders and that deterrence rationale rests on the abandoned assumption that individuals think before they act).

367 PRINCIPLED SENTENCING: READING ON THEORY AND POLICY 90(Andrew Von Hirsch & Andrew Ashworth ed.,) (2d. ed. 1998).

368 Ronald J. Rychlak, *Society's Moral Right to Punish: a Further Exploration of the Denunciation Theory of Punishment*, 65 Tul. L. Rev 299,312-313(1990).

unaware of his actions, including their consequences, the circumstances, and the penalty imposed upon violating the social moral code, does not demonstrate a challenge or unwillingness to comply with that code in the future. Thus, he cannot be punished under the incapacitation rationale.

The rehabilitation rationale focuses on reforming hostile individuals so that they will refrain from offending in the future.[369] The application of rehabilitation ideology is limited to individuals who knowingly express their hostility toward society. Therefore, an individual who is unaware of the prohibitory norm concerning his actions and their consequences and the attending circumstances is not a candidate for rehabilitation because he is not a "truly hostile" individual.

The denunciation rationale maintains that criminal sanction serves an important function of "denouncing" criminal conduct.[370] Enumerating the prohibitory norms will not suffice; rather the offender must be punished.[371] By punishing the offender the society announces a condemnation statement toward the offender's offensive conduct. Accordingly, if an agent is either unaware of the prohibition of his actions, the nature or quality of his actions and their consequences, or the attending circumstances, he cannot be held morally blameworthy. As a result, the society should not condemn his "uninformed" actions.

The retribution theory claims that we should punish offenders because they deserve to be punished, even though the punishment produces no other benefits.[372] Obviously, the agent whose knowledge is impaired due to a lack of awareness of the nature and quality of his actions, their consequences, the attending circumstances, or the prohibitory norms is not morally culpable. Thus, the punishment is unwarranted.

Finally, the educational function of punishment maintains that law educates the general public throughout the process of habit forming.[373] The law educates the public by endorsing good habits that conform to the social moral code and eradicating bad habits that contradict it.[374] Consequently, the law creates a tendency to exercise beneficial habits and refrain from harmful habits.[375] However, the crucial requirement for habit forming is knowledge. An individual may abstain from a harmful conduct, which is a potential bad habit, if he knows that that a particular conduct under particular circumstances will cause

---

[369] HERBERT L. PACKER, THE LIMITS OF THE CRIMINAL SANCTION 53 (1968). For further analysis to the rehabilitation rationale *See* PAUL H. ROBINSON, CRIMINAL LAW 14-15 (1997).
[370] Henry Hart, *The Aims of The Criminal Law*, 23 Law & Contemp. ProBs, 401, 418 (1958).
[371] NIGEL WALKER, PUNISHMENT DANGER AND STIGMA 28 (1980).
[372] MICHAEL MOORE, PLACING BLAME 153-154(1997).
[373] LEON PETRAZYCKI, LAW AND MORALITY 301(Hugh W. Babb trans., Harvard University press .1955).
[374] *Id.*
[375] *Id.*

a harmful result. Similarly, an individual may be encouraged to perform good conduct, which is a potential good habit, if he knows that the conduct is permitted or at least tolerated. Therefore, lack of knowledge precludes habit formation. Accordingly, the educational function of the punishment fails in the absence of essential knowledge.

The forgoing conclusion is that in the absence of knowledge, punishment is not justified, since knowledge is an indispensable requirement in every punishment rationale. If knowledge were not required in at least one rationale, the courts could punish relying upon this rationale. Yet, knowledge is a prerequisite of the six punishment rationales. Therefore, in the absence of knowledge, the courts lose the *moral power* to punish.

The second argument that supports knowledge as the *source* of culpability is a constitutional one. It is based upon the United States Supreme Court's interpretation of the Due Process Clause and the proportionality doctrine. As an implied requirement of the Eighth Amendment, the United States Supreme Court has had a long tradition of requiring proportionality between a defendant's blameworthiness and the punishment.[376] The proportionality doctrine takes into account not only the injury caused by the crime but also the "moral depravity" or "moral blameworthiness" of the defendant.[377] Thus, a defendant cannot be convicted consistently with the proportionality doctrine if there is no evidence of moral blameworthiness. How blameworthy is the defendant who lacked knowledge? Obviously the defendant who did not know either the nature of his acts, their possible consequences, or the attending circumstances is not blameworthy.

It should be noted that the proportionality doctrine is merely a restatement of a deeply rooted measure of culpability. Long before the United States Supreme Court's recognition of the proportionality doctrine, the relationship between moral culpability and punishment was realized. The law realizes that we should not punish the insane, not because of their disability but for their lack of understanding. The law created the mistake defense to excuse faulty knowledge. Knowledge is the law's primary requirement to form culpable choice. When knowledge is lacking, there is neither culpable choice, nor blameworthiness, nor just punishment.

---

[376] Solem v. Helm, 463 U.S. 277, 286 (1983); Weems v. United States, 217 U.S. 349 (1910); O'Neil v. Vermont, 144 U.S. 323, 339-340 (1892) (Field, J., dissenting); It should be noted that Stanford v. Kentucky (492 U.S. 361 (1989)) and Payne v. Tennessee (501 U.S. 808(1991)) decisions may seem to challenge the basic foundations of the proportionality doctrine. However, it is obvious that United States Supreme Court did not abrogate the doctrine of proportionality altogether; rather it allowed other considerations that may conflict with the general rule of proportionality. See Payne v. Tennessee, 501 U.S. 808,825-828 (1991) (In assessing the defendant's blameworthiness at a capital sentencing hearing the court allowed evidence and argument relating to the victim and the impact of the victim's death on the victim's family.)

[377] Coker v. Georgia 433 U.S. 584,598(1977).

Constructing knowledge as a requirement of Due Process can be puzzling. In some cases, the United States Supreme Court emphasized the need for knowledge as a requirement of Due Process.[378] The court shows reluctance in construing a statute without integrating knowledge within the offense.[379] Furthermore, the court burdened Congress with the explicit elimination of the knowledge element if it so desired.[380] The implied suggestion is that there is a strong presumption of the existence of the knowledge element in every offense.[381] Such a presumption can be rebutted only by explicit legislative statement. This mode of analysis encourages some state courts to require knowledge as a matter of constitutional suitability.[382]

However, the United States Supreme Court, in *Baker v. Missouri,* [383] suggested the opposite conclusion. The defendant was convicted of capital murder of the victim, who was a police officer assigned as an undercover agent and dressed in street clothes at the time of the shooting. At the sentencing phase, the jury was instructed that it may impose the death penalty if it found that the murder "was committed against a peace officer while engaged in the performance of his official duty." The jury was not instructed that it also had to find that the defendant knew or should have known that the victim was a police officer. The jury imposed the sentence of death solely on the basis of this aggravating circumstance. The court denied the defendant's certiorari. Justice Marshal in the dissent raised a number of sound concerns. He observed that the identity of the victim is relevant to the defendant's blameworthiness only when it is known to him.[384] Additionally, the goal of deterrence is not advanced since penalty enhancement for killing a police officer could not deter an individual who is ignorant of the identity of his victim.[385]

Some state courts adopted a similar perspective to the one stated in *Baker*. In *People v. Young,*[386] the defendant came upon a struggle between a teenaged boy and two men, finding the boy struggling tearfully and ineffectually. In the defendant's attempt to rescue the boy from the attackers, the

---

[378] Lambert v. California, 355 U.S.225, 229-230(1957)(The court noted that a person cannot be convicted consistently with Due Process where there is no proof of the probability of knowledge of a legal duty)

[379] Staples v. United States, 511 U.S. 600 (1994)(The court required, as an implied element of the offense, the defendant's knowledge of the character of the gun.)

[380] *Id.* at 616

[381] Morissette v. United States, 342 U.S. 246, 250 (1952)(The Court rejected the notion that omission of mention of criminal intent from a statute dispenses with the requirement.)

[382]Estes v. Commonwealth ,952 S.W. 2d 701,703 (KY.1997)(The court concluded, "The imposition of absolute liability on an operator of a motor vehicle where he does not have some knowledge element is unconstitutional as a criminal penalty cannot be applied if a person has no knowledge of the duty owed.")

[383]Baker v. Missouri, 459 U.S. 1183 (1983).

[384] *Id.* at 1186-1187.

[385] *Id.* at 1187-1188.

[386] People v. Young, 210 N.Y.S.2d 358, 11 N.Y.2d 247(1962).

leg of one of the attackers was broken. In actuality, the attackers were police officers arresting the boy for disorderly conduct. The defendant was charged with assault, whereupon he raised the issue of mistake of fact. The court of appeal rejected his claim, stressing the importance of safeguarding police officers; the dissenters argued that such a holding would discourage individuals from assisting their fellow human beings.

The decisions of *Baker*[387] and *Young*[388] deserve vigilant examination. In both cases the only rationale supporting the decision is the legislative intent to safeguard police officers engaged in the performance of their official duty. This rationale, however, fails, as Justice Marshal observed, in that a defendant ignorant of the identity of a police officer cannot be deterred.[389] On the other hand, the shortcomings of such a penal policy are remarkable. Punishing or enhancing the punishment for an unknown fact or a fact that could not have been known is likely to cause social demoralization. In some cases, as in the *Young* case, this penal policy would discourage individuals from appropriate and encourageable conduct. It would convey the wrong message to the public. The message would be that the criminal justice system is unjust because it punishes, or enhances the punishment of, individuals for unknown facts or facts that could not have been known. However, if the defendant knew or should have known the facts and committed the offense nonetheless his informed disobedience, solely, provides an independent basis for blameworthiness, justifying social condemnation.[390]

So far as the constitutionality of knowledge as a requirement of Due Process is concerned, the *Baker* decision should not be overestimated. The Court in *Baker*[391] never discussed the relationship between knowledge of a fact and Due Process, given that the *Baker* decision was merely an unreasoned certiorari denial. In this context, the earlier jurisprudence established in *Lambert,*[392] *Staples,*[393] and *Morissette*[394] prevails in requiring knowledge as indispensable requirement of Due Process.

The doctrine of lenity plays a decisive role in construing knowledge as a requirement of Due Process. It requires the courts to resolve any ambiguity

---

[387] Baker v. Missouri, 459 U.S. 1183 (1983).

[388] People v. Young, 210 N.Y.S.2d 358, 11 N.Y.2d 247(1962).

[389]JEREMY BENTHAM, THE UTILITARIANS: AN INTRODUCTION TO THE PRINCIPLES OF MORALS AND LEGISLATION 164(Dolphin Books Doubleday & company, Inc. Garden City, New York (1961)(Jeremy Bentham concluded that the punishment is not effective for the offenders who commit the prohibited conduct because of temporary lack of control or knowledge in relation to a particular act).

[390] Henry Hart, *The Aims of the Criminal Law*, 23 Law & Contemp. ProBs., 401, 418 (1958).

[391] Baker v. Missouri, 459 U.S. 1183 (1983).

[392] Lambert v. California, 355 U.S.225, 229-230(1957).

[393] Staples v. United States, 511 U.S. 600 (1994).

[394] Morissette v. United States, 342 U.S. 246, 250 (1952).

concerning the criminal statute in favor of lenity.[395] Thus, when the courts confront two contradictory views, such as *Baker*[396] on the one hand and *Lambert,*[397] *Staples,*[398] and *Morissette*[399] on the other, the courts should resolve the contradicted jurisprudence in favor of lenity. Certainly the lenity doctrine would demand the lenient jurisprudence established in *Lambert*, *Staples,* and *Morissette,* that knowledge is an indispensable requirement in every offense unless the legislature explicitly states otherwise.

Apart from constitutional and punishment justification arguments, the overwhelming majority of jurists and courts agree upon the inevitability of knowledge as a source of criminal liability. The proposition is that, generally, *mens rea* is required in every offense.[400] To form *mens rea* there must be some fault.[401] A person cannot be at fault without some degree of understanding of the facts and circumstances as well as some degree of awareness of the result of the intended act.[402] The mental process of such understanding involves the use of

---

[395] Rewis v. United States, 401 U.S. 808, 812 (1971); United States v. United States Gypsum Co., 438 U.S. 422, 437 (1978); United States v. Bass, 404 U.S. 336, 347-348 (1971); Bell v. United States, 349 U.S. 81, 83 (1955); United States v. Universal C. I. T. Credit Corp., 344 U.S. 218, 221-222 (1952); Bifulco v. United States, 447 U.S. 381, 387 (1980); Crandon v. United States, 110 S. Ct. 997 (1990).

[396] Baker v. Missouri, 459 U.S. 1183 (1983).

[397] Lambert v. California, 355 U.S.225, 229-230(1957).

[398] Staples v. United States, 511 U.S. 600 (1994).

[399] Morissette v. United States, 342 U.S. 246, 250 (1952).

[400] *See, e.g.*, Dennis v. United States, 341 U.S. 494,500, 71 S.Ct. 857, 862, (1951) (holding that "[t]he existence of a mens rea is the rule, rather than the exception to, the principles of Anglo-American jurisprudence."). *See also* United States v. United States Gypsum Co., 438 U.S. 422, 436-437, 57 L. Ed. 2d 854, 98 S. Ct. 2864 (1978)(The court reasserted the requirement of some *mens rea* within the definition of every offense.). United States v. Nofziger, 878 F.2d 442, 452 (D.C.Cir.1989).

[401] *See, e.g.*, Morissette v. United States, 342 U.S. 246, 250, 96 L. Ed. 288, 72 S. Ct. 240 (1952) (The court has indicated a dislike of a criminal conviction absent the fault element). H. L .A. HART, PUNISHMENT AND RESPONSIBILITY 40 (1968) (suggesting that the punishment is just only if it involves wrongful culpable choice). The Queen v. Tolson 23 Q.B.D 168,172 (1889)(Wills J) (holding that the guilty intent is not necessarily that intending the very act or thing done and prohibited by common or statutory law, but it must at least be the intention to do something wrong). A.P. Simester & A.T.H. Smith, Criminalization and The Role of Theory, *in* HARM AND CULPABILITY 6 (A.P. Simester & A.T.H. Smith ed., 1996)("Criminalization of harms cannot be accounted for without reference to fault...."). *See also* Morissette v. United States, 342 U.S. 246,250(Jackson J.)

[402] *See* Lynch v. D.P.P [1975] 1 ALL E.R. 913 (Lord Simon asserted that "The general basis for criminal responsibility is the power of choice involved in the axiomatic freedom of the human being."). Samuel H. Pillsbury, *Crimes of Indifference*, 49 Rutgers L. Rev. 105, 123(1996) (Professor Pillsbury emphasized that "the notion that culpability depends on awareness of risk is no passing fancy of the law. Moral arguments of many kinds turn on the assumption that the individual's awareness of certain facts determines responsibility....")

knowledge and reasoning.[403] Thus, as a general rule, knowledge is required in every *mens rea*.

In sum, knowledge is a fundamental concept justifying punishment, a constitutional necessity of Due Process and the proportionality doctrine, and an indispensable requirement of *mens rea*.

C. HISTORICAL OVERVIEW OF KNOWLEDGE: THE FOUR PRONGS OF KNOWLEDGE

The concept of knowledge played a major role in forming the philosophy of criminal responsibility. It was suggested that the lack of knowledge or the mistaken belief of a fact renders any act morally involuntary.[404] Therefore, when knowledge is lacking or erroneous, the defendant is entitled to a mistake defense, which, in turn, negates the mental element of the crime.[405]

Historically, the concept of knowledge has been divided into four prongs, namely, knowledge of the law, knowledge of the circumstances, knowledge of the result, and knowledge of the nature of the act. These prongs have been recognized, to a certain extent, to be the essential requirements of culpability.[406] Therefore, it is necessary to explore their nature and limitations.

The old maxim, ignorance of law is no excuse, suggests that knowledge of law is presumed. However, this rule tolerates some exceptions. If the defendant could not have knowledge of the prohibition because notice of the statute could not reach him, then he should be excused.[407] Although the majority of courts do not excuse a defendant because of lack of knowledge of law, it is considered as a mitigating factor during sentencing.[408]

Some degree of awareness of the result "causing death" has been typically required in homicide cases. A number of tests have been applied to assess the defendant's awareness. While some cases required an actual

---

[403] DAVID ABRAHAMSEN, CRIME AND THE HUMAN MIND 184 (1944). Leland v. Oregon, 343 U.S. 790,800(1952) (concluding that knowledge of right and wrong is the exclusive test of criminal responsibility in a majority of American jurisdictions).

[404] 1 MATHEW HALE, THE HISTORY OF THE PLEAS OF THE CROWN 42 (1847) (stating that "in some cases *ignorantia facti* does excuse, for such an ignorance many times makes the act itself morally involuntary").

[405] Regina v. Tolson 23 Q.B.D 168 (1889).

[406] While knowledge of law is usually presumed, an awareness of the nature, character, and consequences of the conduct is the basis of criminal liability. If any of the three is not present a defendant might be acquitted under defense of insanity. *See Regina* v. Oxford. 9 Car. & P. 525.

[407] Regina v. Bailey, Russ.& Ry.1, 168 Eng.Rep.651(1800)

[408] *See* Regina. v. Esop 7 Car. & P. 456, 173 Eng.Rep.203 (1836) (holding that "It is no defense on behalf of a foreigner charged in England with a crime committed there, that he did not know he was doing wrong. The act not being an offense in his country. But though it is not a defense in law, yet it is matter to be consider in mitigating of punishment")

awareness of death,[409] others imposed a reasonableness standard,[410] or reasonable likelihood of causing death as a result of the defendant's conduct.[411] The seventeenth-century case of *Levett* illustrates the significance of knowledge of the circumstances in shaping culpability.[412] In this case the defendant killed the victim mistakenly believing that she was a burglar.[413] He was acquitted on the grounds of lack of knowledge of the circumstances.[414]

Regarding knowledge of the nature of the act, the early authorities recognized that a crime is not committed unless intent to injure exists.[415] To form such an intent an actor must possess the capacity to know[416] and be able to distinguish between good and evil;[417] accordingly, he can appreciate the nature

---

[409] Regina v. Walters 174 Eng. Rep. 455 (1841) (Coltman J.) (He states "If the circumstances are not such that the party must have been aware that the result would be death" the crime would not be murder rather, at most manslaughter.)

[410] *See* Regina v. Whitmarsh (1898) 62 J.P.1711 (the judge directed the jury that the killing was murder unless the prisoner as reasonable man could have no possibility of death in his act) *followed in* Regina v. Bottomly and Earnshaw(1903) 115 L.T.J. 88.

[411] *See* Vamplew 176 Eng. Rep. 234 (1862)(Pollock C. B. directed the jury that no one could commit murder without "consciousness that the act done would be likely to cause death"). Regina v. Serne, 16 Cox 311 (1887)(Stephen J directed the jury that conduct "which, to the defendant's knowledge, was likely to cause death"). Regina v. Thorpe 168 Eng. Rep. 1001 (1829)(Bayley J stated "if the defendant action is exceedingly dangerous (as in reckless indifference cases) it is likely that Jury will convict for murder."). *See also* EDWARDO COKE, 3 THE INSTITUTE OF THE LAWS OF ENGLAND 56 (1797)56 (stating that "If a man knowing that many people come in the street from sermon, throw a stone over a wall, intending only to fear them or to give them light hurt and there upon one is killed, this is a murder, for he had ill intent, though that intent extended not to death and though he knew not the party slain")

[412] Regina. v. Levett, (1639) Cro.Car.538.

[413] *Id.*

[414] *Id., see also* ROBERT CHAMPERS, 1 A COURSE OF LECTURES ON THE ENGLISH LAW 333 (1767-1773) (Thomas M. Curleyed ed.) (Stating "A third species of ignorance, not natural like the former two, but accidental, is ignorance of event, *when one thing is intended and another effected* as when a fowler shooting at a bird in hedge kills a man behind it. This is called causality or misfortune. As all guilt consists in the will no man can properly by guilty of that which he does not will. If therefore the action itself be lawful or indifferent and the consequent mischief apparently un-designed and not to be foreseen, it is not considered criminal").

[415] 2 BRACTON ON THE LAWS AND CUSTOMS OF ENGLAND 384 (SAMUEL E. THORNE ed., Harvard University Press 1968).

[416] Regarding the requirement of capacity to know to commit an offense *See* EDWARDO COKE, 3 THE INSTITUTE OF THE LAWS OF ENGLAND 54 (1797) (He stated "if a man lose his memory by the rage of sickness or infirmity or otherwise and kill himself while he is not Compos Mentis he is not *felo de se*: for as he cannot commit murder upon another so in that case he cannot commit murder upon himself")

[417] Regarding the requirement of knowledge of good and evil *See* MICHAEL DALTON, COUNTRY JUSTICE 223 (1619)(He states "if one that is non compos mentis, or an idiot, kill a man; this is no felony; for they have no knowledge of good and evil, nor can have felonious intent, nor a will or mind to do harm: and no felony or murder can be

and quality of his conduct. In this context, any defect of knowledge (or understanding) constitutes a defect of will, which precludes liability.[418]

D. THE MODERN APPLICATION OF KNOWLEDGE PRONGS

The courts and legislative bodies developed the four prongs of knowledge to be one of the most essential bases for liability in modern thought. Yet, there are noticeable variations in the application and degree of recognition of the four prongs. It is necessary to explore each prong individually, examining its interpretation while analyzing the validity of its recognition or denial.

1. Knowledge of the Circumstances in Statutory Construction

Knowledge of the circumstances is either an essential factor integrated into the nature of the fact of the killing[419] or an aggravating factor that elevates the degree of the offense. Thus, when a defendant knew that he was setting fire to an occupied apartment building—and realized that such conduct carried with it the risk of death to the occupants—the knowledge of the occupancy of the building was a circumstance relevant, or determinative, to his liability.[420]

The state courts have adopted contradictory approaches with respect to knowledge of the circumstances, specifically with respect to aggravating circumstances. The majority of states require the defendant's knowledge of the aggravating circumstances.[421] However, some states deliberately exclude it. Massachusetts' courts maintain that murder committed with malice aforethought

---

committed without a felonious intent & purpose; for it is called '*Felonia quia fieri debet felleo animo*'") *Id.*

[418] *See* Sir WILLIAM BLACKSTONE, 4 COMMENTARIES ON THE LAWS OF ENGLAND 21 (1800) (He stated, "Now there are three cases, in which the will does not join with the act: 1. Where there is a defect of understanding, for where there is no discernment, there is no choice; and where there is no choice, there can be no act of the will which is nothing else but a determination of one's choice to do or to abstain from particular action: he therefore, that has no understanding, can have no will to guide his conduct. 2. Where there is understanding and will sufficient, residing in the party, but not called forth and exerted at the time of the action done; which is the case of all offenses by chance or ignorance. Here the will fits neuter; and neither concurs with the act, nor disagrees to it.")

[419] *See* People v. Derrera 667 P.2d 1363(Colo.1983)(overruling defective jury instruction defining "knowingly" with respect to result but not the nature of the conduct and the attending circumstances)

[420] Commonwealth v. Mello, 420 Mass. 375; 649 N.E.2d 1106 (Mass.1995).

[421] Cook v. State, 884 S.W.2d 485 (TX.1994) (holding that "Section 19.03(a) (1) requires not just an intent to cause a particular result, e.g., the death of a peace officer or fireman, but also requires that the defendant have knowledge of the circumstances surrounding the conduct, e.g., that the defendant also know the complainant is a peace officer or a fireman"). *See also* New York penal code § 125.27 and Ohio R. C. 2901.22(B).

may be found to have been committed with extreme atrocity or cruelty, although the defendant did not know that his act was extremely atrocious or cruel.[422] However, the same courts insist that knowledge of the circumstances is a determinative factor to infer the existence of malice aforethought.[423]

The distinction between knowledge of the circumstances as a determinative for liability and knowledge of the circumstances as aggravating circumstances is unfounded. The doctrine of proportionality maintains that the punishment is not just unless it is relevant to the defendant's moral blameworthiness. A defendant is not blameworthy unless he made a culpable choice. A culpable choice necessarily requires knowledge of the facts, circumstances, and so on. Therefore, malice and the aggravating circumstances stand on the same footing, both requiring knowledge. Contending otherwise, as Massachusetts' courts suggest, renders the punishment for the aggravating circumstances unjustified.

If the element of knowledge of the circumstances is not explicitly stated in the statutory drafting, it is the court's task to pronounce it as an implied requirement of culpability for the reasons explained earlier. The United States Supreme Court, in a number of cases, presented this proposition. In *Morissette,*[424] the defendant was a scrap collector who removed spent shell casings from a federal bombing range while on a hunting expedition, believing them to be refuse in which the government no longer had any interest. The trial court instructed the jury that it had to find only that Morissette intended to take the property without any reference to the "knowledge of conversion" simply because such knowledge was not expressly stated as a requirement. The United States Supreme Court firmly rejected the notion that omission of mention of the criminal intent from a statute dispenses with an intent requirement.[425] The Supreme Court created a presumption that in the absence of *mens rea* in a

---

[422] Commonwealth v. Lawrence, 404 Mass. 378, 393-394, 536 N.E.2d 571 (1989); Commonwealth v. Sinnott, 399 Mass. 863, 879, 507 N.E.2d 699 (1987); Commonwealth v. Golston, 373 Mass. 249, 260, 366 N.E.2d 744 (1977), cert. denied, 434 U.S. 1039, 54 L. Ed. 2d 788, 98 S. Ct. 777 (1978); Commonwealth v. Appleby, 358 Mass. 407, 415, 265 N.E.2d 485 (1970); Commonwealth v. Gilbert, 165 Mass. 45, 42 N.E. 336 (1895).

[423] Commonwealth v. Chance, 174 Mass. 245, 252, 54 N.E. 551, 554 (1899); Commonwealth v. Starling, 382 Mass. 423, 428, 416 N.E.2d 929, 932 (1981); Commonwealth v. Swift, 382 Mass. 78, 83, 413 N.E.2d 717, 719 (1980); Commonwealth v. Judge, 420 Mass. 433, 650 N.E.2d 1242 (1995).

[424] Morissette v. United States, 342 U.S. 246, 72 S.Ct. 240 (1952). *See also* Liparota v. United States, 471 U.S. 419 (A restaurant owner was convicted of violating a federal statute prohibiting the use or transfer of food stamps. The United States Supreme Court required knowledge of illegality as an essential element of the offense, despite the absence of any language in the statute indicating such a requirement). Morissette was followed by a number of decisions support its findings *see* United States v. United States Gypsum Co., 438 U.S. 422, 438 (1978).

[425] Morissette v. United States, 342 U.S. 246,250, 72 S.Ct. 240, 243

statute, the courts should construe the statute in concert with traditional jurisprudence prerequisites.[426]

2. Knowledge of the Consequences: The Necessity of Knowledge of the Consequences

Traditionally Common Law regards knowledge of the consequences of a conduct that might (or will) cause death, when the act is unlawful, as a species of implied malice or presumed malice.[427] Although acting with the mere knowledge of the consequences of death is not intentional homicide in the narrowest sense, it has been considered the equivalent of purposeful killing, given that the actor who is certain that death will ensue because of his conduct is as culpable as the actor who desires it.[428] Yet, knowledge of the consequences is a matter of degree. It ranges from certainty of the occurrence of the consequences to high probability to mere probability. In this context, the courts and legislative bodies require various degrees of knowledge to incur liability. In general terms, if the knowledge of the risk of death is that it is merely probable, one is *likely* to classify the defendant's state of mind as reckless.[429] If the

---

[426] *Id.* at 342 U.S. 246,263, 72 S. Ct. 240, 250 (The court held: "[W]here Congress borrows terms of art in which are accumulated the legal tradition and meaning of centuries of practice, it presumably knows and adopts the cluster of ideas that were attached to each borrowed word in the body of learning from which it was taken and the meaning its use will convey to the judicial mind unless otherwise instructed. In such case, the absence of contrary direction may be taken as satisfaction with widely accepted definitions, not as a departure from them").

[427] RAY MORELAND, THE LAW OF HOMICIDE 16 (1952). *See also* Achey v. State, 64 Ind. 56(Ind.1878); State v. Sullivan, 51 Iowa 142; 50 N.W. 572; (Iowa .1879), People v. Fish, 125 N.Y. 136; 26 N.E. 319; (1891 N.Y).

[428] Walter Dickey, David Schultz and James L. Fullin, *The Importance of Clarity In The Law Of Homicide: The Wisconsin revision,* 1989 Wis. L. Rev. 1323, 1337. For an accurate statement of the history of common law *See* WILLIAM HAWKINS, 1 A TREATISE OF THE PLEAS OF THE CROWN 39 (1824)(He states, "Neither shall he be adjudged guilty of a less crime who kills another in doing such a willful act as shows him to be as dangerous as a wild beast, and an enemy to mankind in general; as by going deliberately with a horse used to strike, or discharge a gun among a multitude of people, or throwing a great stone or piece of timber from a house into the street, through which he knows that many are passing; and it is no excuse that he intended no harm to any one in particular, or that he meant to do it only for sport, or to frighten the people &c…"). *See also* United States v. United States Gypsum Co,438 U.S.442 ,445 (1978)(The United States Supreme Court suggested that in most crimes there is limited distinction between knowledge and purpose, which has not been considered important, since there is good reason for imposing liability whether the defendant desired or merely knew for practical certainty of the results).

[429] Jeremy M. Miller, *Mens Rea Quagmire: The Conscience Or Consciousness Of The Criminal Law?* 29 W.St.U.L.Rev.21,31. GLANVILLE WILLIAMS, TEXT BOOK OF CRIMINAL LAW 96 (2d ed .1983)(Professor Williams concluded that recklessness

knowledge of the risk of death is that it is certain to occur, one is *likely* to classify the defendant's state of mind as intentional homicide, which includes the common law state of mind of "malice aforethought"[430] and "knowingly" as construed by a number of states.[431]

Although some degree of knowledge of the consequences seems a natural and logical[432] requirement in the most serious offense of homicide, some legislatures overlook its importance either intentionally or as a result of defective statutory drafting. Some statutes criminalize particular conducts exclusive of any degree of knowledge of the consequences. For instance, first-degree reckless homicide in Wisconsin is satisfied by causing the death of a person as a result of unlawful manufacturing, distributing, or delivery of controlled substance.[433] No reference whatsoever is made to a mental state that incorporates any degree of knowledge of the consequences of death. The question then arises: can a defendant be held blameworthy for unknown result? The obvious answer is that, if the defendant did not know and could not know the result of his conduct, he is not blameworthy as to the unknown results. Thus, the defendant who is not blameworthy for particular results cannot be punished for those results; otherwise the proportionality doctrine is violated.[434]

"normally involves conscious and unreasonable risk-taking either as to the possibility that a particular undesirable circumstances exists or to the possibility that some evil will come to pass").

[430] Current English law requires for a murder charge the test of "foresight of virtual certainty" *See* Regina v. Moloney [1985] 1 All ER 1025; Regina v. Nedrick [1986] 3 All ER 1, [1986] 1 WLR 1025. *See also* ALAN NORRIE, CRIME REASON AND HISTORY 50-56 (2ed edition 2001). *See also* EDWARDO COKE, 3 THE INSTITUTE OF THE LAWS OF ENGLAND 56(1797) (He states, "If a man knowing that many people come in the street from sermon, throw a stone over a wall, intending only to fear them or to give them light hurt and their upon one is killed, this is a murder, for he had ill intent, though that intent extended not to death and though he knew not the party slain").

[431] Some states rejected the Model Penal Code scheme of "high probability" of the knowledge of the consequences requiring actual knowledge. *See* State v. Nations 676 S.W.2d 282,285 (Missouri); ILCS 5/4-5(b)(2002) (Illinois). In fact, knowledge requires actual awareness of circumstances rather than their probability, as the Model Penal Code argues. See Ira P. Robins, *Criminal Law: The Ostrich Instruction: Deliberate Ignorance as A Criminal Mens Rea,* 81 J. Crim. L. & Criminology 191,222-223(1990).

[432] Henderson v. Kibbe, 431 U.S. 145,156(1977) (holding that "the jury's determination that the respondent acted recklessly necessarily included a determination that the ultimate harm was foreseeable to him"). United States v. Escamilla 467 F.2d 341, 346 (4th Cir.1972) (holding that "as a necessary element of involuntary manslaughter by the commission of a lawful act without due caution and circumspection, that defendant must be shown to have actual knowledge that his conduct was a threat to the lives of others."). D.W. Elliot, *Offences against the Person-Murder* [1977] Crim.L.Rev.70, 74-75, 77 (Professor Elliot concluded, "Risk taking definition does not suffice without knowledge of the result. Lack of knowledge will unjustifiably equate between different levels of culpability 'recklessness and negligence'"). *Id.*

[433] Wis. State. § 940.02(2) (a) & (b) (2002).

[434] Solem v. Helm, 463 U.S. 277, 286 (1983).

Defective statutory drafting appears when a state legislature inadequately explains the element of knowledge of the consequences. In *State v. Page,*[435] the defendant killed the victim by striking him on the head with a baseball bat after a verbal confrontation. In the trial, the instructions did not demand any degree of the awareness of the consequences. In the absence of model jury instructions, the jury was instructed that the defendant was liable for his conduct if he was aware of his conduct *or* the attending circumstances *or* that the conduct was reasonably certain to cause the result (death). Eventually, the defendant was convicted in the trial. The court of criminal appeal reversed the conviction, advising the legislative bodies to draft pattern jury instructions that include knowledge of the conduct *and* the attending circumstances *and* the result of the conduct.[436] However, the problem is not merely erroneous instructions. If the legislature requires knowledge of the consequences as a necessary ingredient of the offense, the trial court, as a matter of constitutional suitability, is required to instruct the jury of the essential points of proving knowledge of the consequences beyond a reasonable doubt.[437] The problem rests in the very broad definition of "knowledge," which can be very easily satisfied, virtually securing a conviction, in every case. For instance, the mental element of second-degree murder in Tennessee is "a knowing killing of another."[438] To define "knowing killing" the trial judge must apply the general provision of culpability, including the definition of "knowingly." The Tennessee Penal Code defines "knowingly" as follows:

---

[435] State v. Page, 81 S.W.3d 781 (Tenn.2002).

[436] Remarkably, when the courts in a number of jurisdictions were faced with identical instructions, they reached similar conclusions to the one stated in *Page. See, e.g.,* Cook v. State, 884 S.W 2d 485,490(Tex. Crim. App) (finding error in injury instructions on murder and voluntary manslaughter, both of which are result-of-conduct offenses, which did not limit "intentionally and knowingly" to result-only language and remanding to court of appeals for harmless error analysis); Barcenes v. State, 940 S.W. 2d 739, 743-744 (Tex.App.1997) (holding defendant charged with murder, a result-of-conduct offense, is entitled to have definitions of "intentionally and knowingly" limited to result-only language, but finding the error harmless); State v. Lambert 280 Mont.231, 929 P.2d 846(1996.Mont) (holding that the trial court incorrectly applied as the mental state of the offense of criminal endangerment the definition of "knowingly" that a defendant need only be aware of his conduct).; People v. Curtis, 627 P.2d 734 (1981.Colo)(holding that the jury instructions on the culpability for extreme indifference killing were defective because they defined "knowingly" with respect to conduct and circumstances but not result); however, some states refuse to extend the mental element "knowingly" to the result, making the defendant guilty of a crime even though there is no degree of awareness required with respect to the result. *See, e.g.,* Alaska Stat. § 11.41.110(a)(2) (2001); Neitzel v. State, 655 P.2d 325 (Alaska Ct.Accp.1983); Abruska v. State 705 P. 2d 1261 (1985.Alas.App).

[437] Francis v. Franklin, 471 U.S. 307(1985) (invalidating jury instruction that states that the acts of a person of a sound mind and discretion are presumed to be the natural and probable consequences of his conduct). *See also* Sandstrom v. Montana 442 U.S.510 (1979).

[438] Tenn. Code Ann. § 39-13-210 (a) (1) (2001).

Knowingly refers to a person which acts knowingly with respect to the conduct *or* to circumstances surrounding the conduct when the person is aware of the nature of the conduct *or* that circumstances exist. A person acts knowingly with respect to a result of the person's conduct when the person is aware that the conduct is reasonably certain to cause the result.[439]

One probable interpretation of the Tennessee code is that second-degree murder is a result-of-conduct offense. Therefore, knowledge of the consequences is a necessary requirement of the offense. However, there are other interpretations, one of which is the trial judge's interpretation in *Page.*[440] With respect to "knowingly," he instructed the jury as follows:

A person acts "knowingly" if that person acts with awareness

(1) That his conduct is of a particular nature; *or*

(2) That particular circumstances exist; *or*

(3) That the conduct was reasonably certain to cause the result.

The requirement of knowingly is also established if it is shown that the defendant acted intentionally.

A person acts intentionally when that person acts with conscious objective or desire either (1) To cause a particular result; *or* (2) To engage in particular conduct.

Remarkably the trial judge followed the statute literally in his instruction. Indeed, the instruction was not erroneous. However, under such instruction, a juror might convict if the defendant engages in a particular conduct (i.e., striking the victim in the head with a baseball bat) without any reference to the actual intention or if the defendant's conduct is of a particular nature (i.e., causing injury to the victim) without any reference to the mental state required. The Tennessee homicide law, in essence, operates as strict liability, since any sort of knowledge or merely causing a particular result is sufficient to convict. In order to avoid these adverse results, the court of criminal appeal replaced "or" with "and"; in other words, the defendant should know the result, the circumstances, AND the nature of his conduct to be guilty of a crime. Nonetheless, the court of appeal's conclusion is far beyond its permissible power of interpreting statutes. It modifies the statute by grouping the various requirements. It seems that the court thought this grouping was a logical necessity to avoid the injustice represented in lowering the requirements of the mental elements to a degree practically equivalent to that of strict liability offenses.

Obviously the legislative bodies are at large to determine the standard of liability for a particular crime.[441] Yet their resolution should not be an

---

[439] Tenn. Code Ann. § 39-13-210 (a) (1) (2001).

[440] State v. Page, 81 S.W.3d 781 (Tenn.2002).

[441] Liparota v. United States, 471 U.S. 419, 424 (1985) (citing United States v. Hudson, 11 U.S. 32, 7 Cranch 32, 3 L. Ed. 259 (1812)). Powell v. State 329 U.S.514, 535-536, 88 S.Ct.2145,2156,20 L.Ed.2d 1254(1968)(holding that "the United States constitution reserves to the states considerable freedom in defining crime, including mental elements required")

arbitrary one. There are always rules and limits for their decision making. The limits are set by our social expectation of the laws that control our behavior. It is very unlikely that our society would convict a person of a capital offense if the person was unaware and could not have been aware of the consequences of his conduct. The degree of knowledge required from individuals must match our expectation. If we presume the existence of knowledge of the consequences[442] in every case, so that individuals are liable for their conduct no matter how careful they are, then individuals may either disregard the threat of the punishment altogether or abandon everyday activities.[443] Those individuals who are unaware and could not have been aware of the consequences of their conducts are unconscious of the applicability of the legal threat to them, rendering general or private deterrence unfeasible.[444] Therefore, if we presume the existence of knowledge of the consequences or require a degree of knowledge higher than that the individuals actually can possess we will lose the deterrent effect of the punishment or unduly restrain our social and economical life. In the context of jury instructions, the best instructions are what the jury believes to be right and reasonable. Otherwise, we will be asking the jurors to make a determination against their intuition. How reasonable could it be to ask the jury to convict if the defendant was unaware and could not have been aware of the consequences of his conduct? If the jury nullifies the law by acquitting the defendant, they are, in fact, not nullifying the law but highlighting the fact that the law was null from the moment of its inception because it did not match our social expectations.

3. Knowledge of the Nature and the Quality of the Conduct: The Existence of Knowledge of the Conduct in the Penal Codes

Most of the states recognize the elements of knowledge of the nature and quality of the conduct *as a necessary element to prove guilt.* Typically they place the burden of proof on the defendant, as in an affirmative defense of insanity.[445]

---

[442] *See* Sandstrom v. Montana, 422 U.S 510(1979) (invalidating instruction stating "the law presumes that a person intended the ordinary consequences of his voluntary acts"); *Followed in* Francis v. Franklin 471U.S.307(1985).

[443] Herbert Wechsler and Jerome Michael, *A Rational of The Law of Homicide* I, 37 Colum. L. Rev 701, 749-750(1937).

[444] *Id.* at 750-751.

[445] *See* M'Naghten Case, 10 Cl.& F.200, 8 Eng. Rep 718(1843); MODEL PENAL CODE § 4.01 (Proposed Official Draft 1962). United States v. Henderson, 680 F. 2d 659,661 (9th Cir.1982); United States v. Smeaton , 762 F.2d 796,799 (9th Cir.1985) (A person is insane if "as result of a mental disease or defect, he lacks substantial capacity to appreciate the wrongfulness of his conduct or to conform his conduct to the requirement of law"). However, the differentiation point that the states disagreed upon is the nature of the knowledge, whether the defendant knows that his conduct was legally or morally wrong. *See, e.g.,* United States v. Fresonke v. 549 F.2d 1253, 1256 (9th Cir.1977) *aff'd in* United States v. Sibley 595 F.2d 1162, 1165-1166 (9th Cir.1979); People v. Skinner 39 Cal.3d 765; 704 P.2d 752 (Cal. 1985) (The conduct must be morally wrong, not legally wrong).

When the legislature omits the element of knowledge of the nature and the quality of the conduct, relying on the affirmative defense of insanity, the legislature not only recognizes the importance of such an element but also eases the prosecution's burden of proof.

As a general rule, knowledge of the nature and quality of the conduct, as a prong of the general scheme of knowledge, is a necessary requirement in every offense for just punishment and a requirement of Due Process and the proportionality doctrine. However, in *Mullaney*,[446] the United States Supreme Court held that if there is logical incompatibility between an affirmative defense and the prosecution's burden of proof of all the elements of the crime charged, such that proof of the affirmative defense negates an element of the offense, the burden of proving such a defense cannot be placed upon the defendant without violating Due Process.[447] Thus, the states cannot place the initial burden of proving *lack* of knowledge of the nature and the quality of the conduct on the defendant in insanity defense, since disproving knowledge negates an element of the offense.[448]

4. Knowledge of Law

The general rule is that knowledge of law is neither a requirement of an offense, nor does its lack constitute a defense.[449] Nonetheless, the courts and legislature on a number of occasions have recognized various exceptions to the general rule.[450] With respect to homicide offenses, knowledge of law is not an issue. The

---

People v. Schmidt 216 N.Y.324; 110 N.E. 945 (1915.N.Y) (the conduct must be legally and morally wrong). State v. Hamann, 285 N.W.2d 180,183 (Iowa. 1979) (the words "right" and "wrong" under M'Naghten rule should be understood in their legal, not in their moral, sense).

[446] Mullaney v. Wilbur, 421 U.S. 684 (1975).

[447] *Id.* at 700-702.

[448] It should be noted that the Patterson decision (Patterson v. New York 432 U.S. 197 (1977)), which validated a statute allocating the burden of persuasion of an affirmative defense to the defendant, does not conflict with Mullaney finding that the state, according to Patterson, must prove every element in the offense.

[449] United States v. Smith, 18 U.S. 153, 5 Wheat. 153, 182, 5 L. Ed. 57 (1820) (Livingston, J., dissenting); Barlow v. United States, 7 Pet. 404, 411 (1833); Reynolds v. United States, 98 U.S. 145, 167, 25 L. Ed. 244 (1879); Shevlin-Carpenter Co. v. Minnesota, 218 U.S. 57, 68, 54 L. Ed. 930, 30 S. Ct. 663 (1910); Lambert v. California, 355 U.S. 225, 228, 2 L. Ed. 2d 228, 78 S. Ct. 240 (1957); Liparota v. United States, 471 U.S. 419, 441, 85 L. Ed. 2d 434, 105 S. Ct. 2084 (1985) (WHITE, J., dissenting); Bryan v. United States, 524 U.S. 184,193(1998).

[450] Lambert v. California 355 U.S.225, 229-230 (reversing conviction and noting that "Where a person did not know of the duty to register and where there was no proof of the probability of such knowledge, he may not be convicted consistently with due process"; Estes v. Commonwealth 952 S.W. 2d 701,703 (KY.1997) relaying on Lambert v. California [355U.S.225 (1957)]. In *Estes* the court held that (the imposition of absolute liability on an operator of a motor vehicle where he does not have some knowledge

idea is that *malum in se* offenses, including homicide offenses, are inherently wrong conducts. Therefore, knowledge of the prohibition is presumed. This connotation is especially true with respect to homicide in that it is impossible to imagine that a person of a sound mind does not know that killing is a wrong conduct.

E. Degrees of Recklessness Instructions

Knowledge of harm is a matter of degree. An actor might be certain of the occurrence of harm or have foreseen the possibility of harm or simply be callous and unconcerned about the possibility of harm. Under the Model Penal Code culpability scheme, these degrees of knowledge are the determinative factor of culpability. If the actor was aware or hoped that harm would occur, the actor acted purposely.[451] If the harm was foreseeable, the actor acted knowingly.[452] If the actor was callous, the actor acted recklessly.[453] Furthermore, the degree of callousness is a decisive factor in culpability.[454] In the context of homicide, if

---

element is unconstitutional, as a criminal penalty cannot be applied if a person has no knowledge of the duty owed.) *Id.* United States v. Ratzlaf 976 F 2d 1280 (The United States Supreme Court construed a statute requiring the "willfully" element to require knowledge not only of the law but also knowledge of illegality of the defendant conduct. However, the court noted that ignorance of law is no excuse). United States v. Obiechie 38 F 3d 309(7th Cir.1994) (The seventh circuit followed Ratzlaf reasoning requiring the government to prove knowledge of illegality to secure conviction under certain federal firearms statutes. In this case the court held that "willfully" must encompass knowledge of illegality). In some occasions, nonpublication of statute may constitute a defense under English law. *See, e.g.,* English Statutory Instrument Act § 3 (2) (1946). *See also* ANDREW ASHWORTH, PRINCIPLES OF CRIMINAL LAW 243(3d ed.1999).

[451] MODEL PENAL CODE § 2.02(2)(a) (Proposed Official Draft 1962).

[452]MODEL PENAL CODE § 2.02(2)(b)& §2.02(7) (Proposed Official Draft 1962).

[453] MODEL PENAL CODE § 2.02(2) (c) (Proposed Official Draft 1962).

[454] The Model Penal Code recklessness grading scheme reflects the correct understanding of the common law history that reckless disregard of human life is a murder rather than manslaughter. See WILLIAM BLACKSTONE, 4 COMMENTARIES ON THE LAWS OF ENGLAND 199-200 (1769) He states:

> [A]s when a park-keeper tied a boy, that was stealing wood, to a horse's tail, and dragged him along the park; when a master corrected his servant with an iron bar, and a schoolmaster stamped on his scholar's belly; so that each of the sufferers died; these were justly held to be murders, because the correction being excessive, and such as could not proceed but from a bad heart, it was equivalent to a deliberate act of slaughter. Neither shall he be guilty of a less crime, who kills another in consequence of such a willful act, as shows him to be an enemy to all mankind in general; as going deliberately with a horse used to strike, or discharging a gun, among a multitude of people .*Id.*

See also A GENERAL VIEW OF THE CRIMINAL LAW OF ENGLAND, JAMES FITZJAMES STEPHEN 115 (1863); 2 BRACTON ON THE LAWS AND CUSTOMS

the actor is merely callous, he is guilty of manslaughter.[455] If the actor is callous as to life or death of others, he is guilty of murder.[456] Until this point the culpability scheme of Model Penal Code is fairly adequate. The problem emerges in the application of these rules when a defendant is charged with reckless homicide. Who is the assessor of the degree of recklessness, the judge or the jury? And if the jury is the appropriate assessor, should the court instruct the jury to the lesser degree of recklessness as a lesser included offense? Indisputably the jury is the appropriate assessor, given that evaluating the degree of recklessness is a factual inquiry. With respect to the instruction on the lesser degree of recklessness, the United States Supreme Court, in *Beck v. Alabama*,[457] held that the Due Process Clause requires that lesser included offense instructions be given only when the evidence warrants such an instruction. However, a defendant is not entitled to have the jury instructed as to lesser degrees of the crime simply because the crime charged is murder.[458] "The decision of whether there is enough evidence to justify a lesser included offense charge rests within the sound discretion of the trial judge."[459]

Perhaps the merit of *Beck*'s rule appears in cases in which the defendant requests instructions on an alternative mental element that is not clearly supported by evidence. For instance, if the evidence suggests killing that was no less than purposeful, the trial judge may decline to instruct on negligent homicide to prevent jury confusion or to avoid a miscarriage of justice by allowing the jury to convict on negligent homicide contrary to the evidence.[460] However, the situation is completely different if there is evidence to support

---

OF ENGLAND 341(SAMUEL E. THORNE ed., Harvard University Press 1968). The modern courts continue to realize that recklessness is a form of implied malice. *See, e.g.*, people v. Philips, 414 P. 2d 353, 363 (Cal. 1966); People v. Thomas, 41 Cal. 2d 470, 480, 261 P. 2d 1, 7 (Cal. 1953); Arave v. Creech 507 U.S. 463, 475 (1993); Regina . v. Sheppard [1981] A.C. 394. A GENERAL VIEW OF THE CRIMINAL LAW OF ENGLAND, JAMES FITZJAMES STEPHEN 83&115 (1863)(Justice Stephen suggested that the common law retain the term "malice aforethought" because it sums up many distinctive mental elements such as reckless indifference). *Compare* Alan Michaels, *Rationales of Criminal Law Then and Now: For a Judgmental Descriptivism*, 100 Colum.L.Rev.54,75(2000) (concluding that that depraved heart murder is "a residual category design to capture reckless killings that were deserving of punishment as intentional").

[455] MODEL PENAL CODE § 2.10.3.(1)(a) (Proposed Official Draft 1962).

[456] MODEL PENAL CODE § 2.10.2(1)(b) (Proposed Official Draft 1962).

[457] Beck v. Alabama 447 U.S. 625(1980), *aff'd in* Hopper v. Evans 456 U.S. 605, 611(1982). *Followed in* Bates v. Lee, 308 F. 3d 411(4th Cir. 2002); Ransom v. Johnson 126 F. 3d 716 (5th Cir. 1997); Mann v. Scott 41 F. 3d 968 (5th Cir. 1994); Campbell v. Coyle 260 F. 3d 531(6th Cir. 2001).

[458] Briley v. Bass, 742 F.2d 155, 164 (4th Cir. 1984).

[459] United States v. Chapman, 615 F.2d 1294 (10th Cir. 1980).

[460] Stirland v. Director of Public Prosecutions [1944] App. Cas. 315, 324. (Lord Viscount Simon concluded, "A miscarriage of justice may arise from the acquittal of the guilty no less than from the conviction of the innocent…").

reckless homicide and the jury's role is to decide not only the existence of recklessness but also its quantum. For instance, when a driver kills while exceeding the speed limit by five miles per hour, it is probable that the driver was merely reckless rather than recklessly indifferent to human life. In contrast, if the driver kills while exceeding the speed limit by fifty miles per hour, it is more probable that the driver was recklessly indifferent to human life. If the driver exceeds the speed limit by ten or fifteen or twenty miles per hour, should we instruct the jury on reckless homicide or reckless indifference to human life or both? Obviously it is a very difficult question to answer, because the quantum of recklessness is a subjective inquiry. Such an inquiry is not and cannot be guided by any rule because it is a question of fact that falls exclusively within the jury's domain.[461]

Furthermore, *Beck*'s judgment suggests that instructions on lesser included offenses have long been recognized to "afford the jury a less drastic alternative than the choice between conviction of the offense and acquittal." In this context, instructing the jury solely on reckless indifference to human life, which satisfies a murder conviction, may drive the jury to acquit the defendant, if the evidence shows some degree of recklessness, but not a sufficient degree to support a reckless indifference conviction.[462] Similarly, a jury instructed on reckless indifference to human life solely may convict the defendant, despite a lack of evidence to support the conviction, because they are reluctant to let the defendant go free.[463] In sum, the discretionary power of the trial court in allowing lesser included offense instructions can be useful in many cases. However, when it involves assessing the quantum of recklessness rather than its suitability as a charge in a particular case, it can be prejudicial and contrary to the rules established in *Beck*.

Given that the prosecutor's charging decisions are almost unreviewable and that the prosecutor may abuse that power for various reasons,[464] the courts

---

[461] However, lesser included offense instructions in reckless homicide as a lesser offense of reckless indifference is very proper, since reckless indifference to human life necessarily includes reckless homicide. *See* Sansone v. United States, 380 U.S. 343,349-350(1965) (A lesser included offense instruction is only proper where the charged greater offense requires the jury to find a disputed factual element that is not required for conviction of the lesser included offense.).

[462]Spaziano v. Florida, 468 U.S. 447, 455 (1984)(holding that "Beck rule's goal is to eliminate the distortion of the fact-finding process that is created when the jury is forced into an all-or-nothing choice between capital murder and innocence.").

[463]Schad v. Arizona, 501 U.S. 624, 646 (1991) (concluding that "Our fundamental concern in Beck was that a jury convinced that the defendant had committed some violent crime but not convinced that he was guilty of a capital crime might nonetheless vote for a capital conviction if the only alternative was to set the defendant free with no punishment at all").

[464] *See* Andrew Horwitz, *Taking the Cop Out of Copping a Plea: Eradicating Police Prosecution of Criminal Cases,* 40 Ariz. L. Rev. 1305, 1317(1998). *See also* Bordenkircher v. Hayes, 434 U.S. 357,364(1978) (stating "[S]o long as the prosecutor has probable cause to believe that the accused committed an offense defined by statute,

should have a tendency to allow lesser included offenses, especially in cases in which there is very fine distinction between the offense charged and the possible charges.[465] Reckless homicide falls into this category of cases because the jury functions are not limited to determining the existence of recklessness but also determine its quantum.

F. The Relationship between the Concept of Unjustified Risk Taking and the Prongs of Knowledge

Recklessness typically requires conscious disregard of unjustified risk.[466] While the factors that render the risk unjustified must be elucidated, it becomes an impossible task given the variability of circumstances. Perhaps the difficulty of defining these justification factors drives the courts to articulate the concept of unjustified risk taking in objective general terms: the defendant is to be held liable as a "law-abiding person in his situation."[467] Thus, embracing objective liability is favored because it relieves the courts of the difficult task of explaining the justification factors. Alternatively, the prongs of knowledge analysis can offer a plausible explanation of the concept of unjustified risk taking. In the context of recklessness, an agent is blameworthy if he is aware that his conduct risks unjustified harm.[468] Thus, the agent must be aware of his conduct, the attending circumstances, the possible consequences, and the law violated. However, knowledge of law must be understood in the broader sense, which exceeds mere knowledge of the statutes and the regulations, to include knowledge of the legal duties in general. Since the well-established jurisprudence affirms that lack of knowledge of law is not a defense, knowledge of law can be understood as knowledge of the legal duties only.[469] The difference between knowledge of law and knowledge of the legal duties is that the latter's scope is much broader and includes numerous uncodified duties that are based upon the common knowledge. For instance, the traffic laws list sanctions for rule violations, however, the paramount legal duty that might be omitted from the traffic laws is driving safely.

The prongs of knowledge illustrate deviations from justified risk taking. For instance, reckless driving leading to death can be classified as

---

the decision whether or not to prosecute, and what charge to file or bring before a grand jury, generally rests entirely in his discretion…").

465 Ironically, some courts have a tendency against allowing lesser included offenses. *See* Ellis v. State, 736 N.E.2d 731(Ind.2000)(The court required that the defendant prove that he acted recklessly to allow the alternative charge; in other words the court not only unconstitutionally shifted the burden of proof but also required the defendant to proof his guilt.)

466 MODEL PENAL CODE § 2.02 (2) (c) (Proposed Official Draft 1962).

467 *Id.*

468 *Id.*

469 *See Smith*, 18 U.S. 153; *Liparota*, 471 U.S. at 441; *Bryan*, 524 U.S. at 193.

manslaughter if it is shown to be mere recklessness,[470] or murder if it denotes reckless indifference to human life.[471] To determine whether the risk is unjustified and to quantitate the degree of risk taking, one can invoke the prongs of knowledge analysis. Thus, exceeding the speed limit by ten miles per hour in a school zone is different from exceeding the speed limit by the same amount on a highway. The knowledge of exceeding the speed limit (knowledge of the act), the knowledge of the legal speed limit (knowledge of the law/knowledge of the legal duties), the knowledge of the circumstances (driving in a school zone or a highway), and the knowledge of the possible consequences (killing a person is more probable in a school zone than on a highway) explain not only the risk that the agent took and its unjustifiability but also the degree of the risk. Accordingly, in the context of jury instructions, invoking the prongs of knowledge to explain the concept of unjustified risk taking is more comprehensible than invoking the hypothetical law-abiding person in the defendant's situation.[472]

IV. ANALYSIS AND CONCLUSION

Part I explained two sets of problems with the definition of "recklessness." The first set demonstrated the theoretically incorrect analysis of recklessness in the jurisdictions that continue to follow the common law. The second set revealed the deficiency in the Model Penal Code's culpability scheme. Although the Model Penal Code distinguishes between reckless homicide and reckless indifference to human life, it falls short of offering guidelines explaining the relationship between reckless homicide and reckless indifference to human life. Such a relationship is of utmost importance in jury instructions because it may or may not demand that reckless homicide is the lesser included offense of reckless indifference to human life.

Part III offered the profound anatomy of recklessness fundamentals, including the prongs of knowledge. It advocated that the prongs of knowledge be the source of criminal culpability. They are not only important in defining recklessness but are also an essential and indispensable requirement in every culpable mental state, including purpose, knowingly, and negligence. Furthermore, we should apply a subjective standard of awareness of risk to avoid constitutional challenges and to avoid injustice arising from overlooking the defendant's special traits that distinguish him from the average person. Because of the difficulty of assessing the degree of knowledge of the consequences, both reckless and reckless indifference homicide must be instructed simultaneously. Finally, knowledge of law is presumed because it is fair to assume that every person of sound mind knows that killing is prohibited

---

[470] MODEL PENAL CODE § 210.3(1) (a) (Proposed Official Draft 1962).
[471] *Id.* § 210.1(1) (b).
[472] *Id.* 2.02 (2) (c).

It should be noted that the fundamentals of recklessness discussed in part III tolerate some variations. Thus, the legislature may raise or lower the degree of knowledge in any prong or attach any qualifier to an element of the offense. Accordingly, under the Model Penal Code's recklessness scheme, the degree of awareness of the possible consequences was increased to become substantial and the risk was qualified as unjustified risk. Similarly, in reckless indifference homicide, the degree of knowledge of the circumstances was increased to show indifference to the value of human life.

V. PROPOSED JURY INSTRUCTIONS

A. INSTRUCTIONS FOR RECKLESS HOMICIDE THAT QUALIFIES FOR MANSLAUGHTER

The defendant is accused of committing reckless homicide (or manslaughter). To convict the defendant, the prosecutor must prove beyond a reasonable doubt that:

1. The defendant was aware of the nature and quality of his conduct. This means not only that the defendant understood what he was doing at the time of committing manslaughter, but that he also appreciated to the fullest what he was doing. The defendant did know that his conduct created unjustified and substantial risk.
2. The defendant was aware of the circumstances that rendered his conduct substantially risky and unjustified.
3. The defendant was aware that death was a possible consequence of his conduct.

B. INSTRUCTIONS FOR RECKLESS INDIFFERENCE HOMICIDE THAT QUALIFIES FOR MURDER

The defendant is accused of committing reckless indifference homicide (or murder). To convict the defendant, the prosecutor must prove beyond a reasonable doubt that:

1. The defendant was aware of the nature and quality of his conduct. This means not only that the defendant understood what he was doing at the time of committing murder, but that he also appreciated to the fullest what he was doing. The defendant did know that his conduct created unjustified and substantial risk. The defendant's conduct manifested extreme indifference to the value of the human life, and the defendant was aware of that fact.
2. The defendant was aware of the circumstances that rendered his conduct substantially risky and unjustified. The circumstances manifest

extreme indifference to the value of the human life, and the defendant was aware of that fact.

The defendant was aware that death was a possible consequence of his conduct. Nevertheless he (or she) did not care that a person(s) might die as a consequence of his conduct.

Chapter Four

Intentional Homicide

I. INTRODUCTION

Nothing is more elusive than understanding the modern legal usage of the concept of intentional killing, because it is employed to describe alternative states of mind.[473] One can start by reviewing the common law concept of malice aforethought, which was reformulated and rephrased in the Model Penal Code. Thus, intentional killing is comprised of two cognitive states of belief—knowledge that the actor's conduct *will* cause death (knowingly), knowledge that the actor's conduct *may* cause death (reckless indifference to human life)—and a state of desire of death (purposely).[474] Since the previous chapter dealt with recklessness, it will not be discussed again in this chapter.

Much of chapter 3 was devoted to the explanation of the concept of knowledge, which forms the core of every cognitive state of belief and is extremely beneficial in illustrating the states of desire. Accordingly, the concept of knowledge will play a major role in this chapter, which will explain the remaining two states of mind of intentional killing that were not discussed in the previous chapter, namely "purposely" and "knowingly."

---

[473] *See* C.T. SISTARE, RESPONSIBILITY AND CRIMINAL LIABILITY 93(1989) (stating, "To intend is taken to mean to design, resolve, propose, plan for, desire or have in mind. Intent may be defined as design, determination, malice, foresight of certain results, foresight of probability or premeditation."). *See, e.g.*, People v. Hood, 462 P.2d, 370,377 (Cal.1969) (concluding that the concepts of general intent and specific intent are "notoriously difficult…to define and apply")

[474] *See* Sandstrom v. Montana 442 U.S.510, 525(1979) (The mental element of intent is much broader than purpose to include awareness and knowledge). *See also* United States v. United States Gypsum Co., 438 U.S. 422, 445 (1978) (holding that [the] element of intent in the criminal law has traditionally been viewed as a bifurcated concept embracing either the specific requirement of purpose or the more general one of knowledge or awareness).

II. THE COGNITIVE STATE OF DESIRE: DESIRE TO CAUSE DEATH VERSUS DESIRE TO CAUSE AN ACT THAT ULTIMATELY CAUSES DEATH

In *Regina v. Steane*,[475] Chief Justice Lord Goddard, in explaining the common law intentional states of mind, distinguishes between two forms of intention. The first is the intention to perform a conduct that ultimately causes death. The second is the intention to cause death. Under correct instruction in the first type of intention, the prosecution may fail to convince the jury of the intention to kill, although the natural consequence of the defendant's act is death. The prosecution's task under the second type of intention is to prove not only the intention to perform the conduct that caused death, but also that the ultimate purpose of the defendant's conduct was death. The significance of this distinction is the recognition that an individual may not intend the natural consequences of his conduct. The United States Supreme Court rearticulated this point in *Sandstrom*,[476] maintaining that the state should not shift the burden of proof by instructing the jury to presume that a person intended the natural consequences of his conduct.

This distinction is of utmost importance with respect to intentional homicide. The states that follow the Model Penal Code's culpability scheme, using various terminologies, correctly require the prosecution to prove that the ultimate purpose of the defendant's conduct was death.[477] In contrast, the majority of the states that continue to follow malice aforethought mental state offer a very broad definition of intentional homicide, merely requiring the prosecution to prove any act that causes death.[478] Limiting the prosecution's task to proving only the act that caused death raises a number of considerations.

---

[475] Regina v. Steane [1947] K.B.997.

[476] Sandstrom v. Montana 442 U.S. 510.

[477] *See* 2 MODEL PENAL CODE AND COMMENTARIES 20-21(Official Draft and Revised Comment. 1980). See also " Wisconsin Penal Code § 939.23(3)("Intentionally" means that the actor either has a purpose to do the thing or cause the result specified, or is aware that his or her conduct is practically certain to cause that result); New Jersey Penal Code § N.J.S.A.2C:22-2b (1)(A person acts purposely with respect to the nature of his conduct or a result thereof if it is his conscious object to engage in conduct of that nature or to cause such a result); Missouri Penal Code § 562.016.2 (A person acts purposely; or with purpose with respect to his conduct or to a result thereof when it is his conscious object to engage in that conduct or to cause the result); Alabama Penal Code § 13A-2-2 (A person acts intentionally with respect to a result or to conduct described by a statute defining an offense, when his purpose is to cause that result or to engage in that conduct.); Alaska Penal Code § AS 11.41.100((a) A person commits the crime of murder in the first degree if (1) with intent to cause the death of another person, the person (A) causes the death of any person").

[478] State v. Mathis, 427 S.W.2d 450, 454 (holding that "'malice aforethought' means 'malice with premeditation; that is, that the unlawful act intentionally done was

First, it constitutes a "very large net" to catch all defendants regardless of their guilt or innocence. It is practically impossible for a defendant to escape conviction under such a definition. If the requirement of the wrongful act alone suffices for a murder conviction, many people can be prosecuted for ordinary wrongful acts that are not homicidal in nature.

Second, the gradations of the punishment scheme offer some incentive to potential offenders to engage in less rather than more undesirable criminal behavior.[479] In satisfying the mental element of murder, only requiring proof of the act that ultimately caused death, while the lesser offense of manslaughter is satisfied by proving recklessness,[480] frustrates the punishment gradation system because the lesser-graded offense of manslaughter bears a higher requirement of culpability than the higher-graded offense of murder.

Third, the United States Supreme Court explicitly warned that very broad definitions of the offenses constitute a violation of the separation of powers doctrine.[481] Clearly, requiring proof of an act exclusive of the true mental state—such as a desire to achieve the result or foreseeing the result or even negligent conduct—is the very broad definition of intentional homicide, which, in turn, renders such a definition unconstitutional.[482]

---

determined upon before it was executed.'"); Mercer v. Commonwealth, 150 Va.588, 142 S.E. 369; Thompson v. Commonwealth, 131 Va.847.109 S.E. 447, Williamson v. Commonwealth 180 Va.227, 23 S.E.2d 240 (holding that malice aforethought "Means any wrongful act done willfully or purposefully and it is presumed from the act of killing, unaccompanied with circumstances extenuation and the burden of disproving malice is upon the accused"); Cook v. State, 511 S.W.2d 877,881 (holding that "'Malice aforethought' is the 'intentional doing of a wrongful act, thought of beforehand."); Gonzalez v. State, 397 S.W.2d 440, 441; Crozier v. State, 723 P.2d 42, 54 (Wyo.1986), followed in Young v. State, 849 P.2d 754,761(Wyo.1993)(holding that "'Malice aforethought' includes all those states of mind under which the killing of a person takes place without any cause which will in law justify, excuse, or extenuate the homicide. It is the doing of a wrongful act intentionally, without just cause or excuse. It is a condition of the mind which shows a heart regardless of social duty and fatally bent on mischief, the existence of which is inferred from acts committed or words spoken."). However, some states offered some specification. *See, e.g.*, Huddleston v. State, 134 Miss. 382, 98 So. 839("malice afterthought" means a deliberate design to kill); Commonwealth v. Delaney, 418 Mass. 658, 661 (Malice may be proven by evidence of any unexcused intent to kill, to do grievous bodily harm, or to do an act creating a plain and strong likelihood that either death or grievous harm would evolve.); Norton v. State, 273 Ind. 635, 534(Ind. 1980) (A killing is done purposely and maliciously when the intention to unlawfully take life is deliberately formed in the mind).

[479] Herbert Wechsler & Jerome Michael, *A Rational of The Law of Homicide II*, 37 Colum. L. Rev 1261, 1266(1937).

[480] Va. Code Ann. § 18.2-36.1 (B) (2002). *See also* Cal Pen Code § 192 (b) (2001) (in the commission of a lawful act that might produce death, in an unlawful manner).

[481] United States v. Reese, 92 U.S.214 (1875).

[482] *Id.* at 221 (holding that "It would certainly be dangerous if the legislature could set a net large enough to catch all possible offenders, and leave it to the courts to step inside

Fourth, intentional homicide is a result-of-offense; therefore, a defendant should not be convicted unless the state proves an act by the defendant and a mental state that establishes the nexus between death and that act. Accordingly, mere proof of the defendant's act defies the crucial, logical definition of intentional homicide as a result-of-offense.

Fifth, to hold a defendant liable for murder merely because his wrongful conduct caused death is either to create an implied presumption that he intended (or was aware of) the consequences of his conduct, or to make murder a strict liability offense because a wrongful act alone, regardless of any state of mind, suffices for conviction. Presuming that the defendant intended the natural consequences of a conduct was expressly rejected by the United States Supreme Court as a matter of constitutional necessity.[483] Considering murder a strict liability offense is an impossible proposition in view of the gravity of the offense. Indeed, states legislatures are entrusted with the definition of offenses and the selection of methodologies to fight crime.[484] However, there is a limit to their powers. They should neither defeat the Due Process Clause by implying that a defendant intended the natural consequences of his acts[485] nor discount justice by casting a very large net to catch all defendants regardless of their innocence, or by considering intentional homicide as a strict liability offense.

In sum, a legislature is at liberty to define the mental states to reflect the community norms and needs. However, there are a number of rules and limits that must be considered. The foundation of the states of desire, particularly intentional homicide, is based upon the prongs of knowledge as explained in the previous chapter. To be liable for intentional homicide, the agent must be aware of nature and quality of his conduct, the attending circumstances, and the consequences of his conduct. The distinctive characteristic of intentional killing, in the narrowest sense, is that the agent aimed for, or desired, the consequences of his conduct. In "reckless indifference to human life" the agent was merely aware of the possibility of death, and nevertheless was callous regarding such possibility.[486] In "knowingly" the agent was practically certain of or at least foresaw the high probability of death as a result of his conduct.[487]

---

and say who could be rightly detained, and who should be set at large. This would to some extent, substitute the judicial for the legislative department of the government.").

[483] Sandstrom v. Montana 442 U.S. 510.

[484] Liparota v. United States, 471 U.S. 419, 424 (1985) (citing United States v. Hudson, 11 U.S. 32, 7 Cranch 32, 3 L. Ed. 259 (1812)).

[485] *See* Sandstrom v. Montana 442 U.S. 510.

[486] MODEL PENAL CODE § 210.2(1) (b) (Proposed Official Draft 1962).

[487] *Id.* § 2.02 (7).

III. THE COGNITIVE STATE OF BELIEF: "KNOWINGLY"

Knowingly, as a cognitive state of belief, is founded on the indispensable prongs of knowledge explained in the previous chapter. Hence, knowingly requires an awareness of the nature and quality of the act, the attending circumstances, and the consequences of the act. This mode of analysis is far from the current interpretation of "knowingly." The majority of jurisdictions, including those that continue to follow common law and those that embraced the Model Penal Code's culpability scheme, integrates one or more of the prongs of knowledge within the definition of "knowingly"[488] and "malice aforethought"[489] or at least maintains that knowledge raises an inference of the intention to kill.[490] However, the integration of the concept of knowledge is neither complete nor principled, which in turn produces unjust results. For instance, in *State v. Frazier*,[491] the defendant struck the victim on the jaw once with his fist. The defendant did not know that the victim was a hemophiliac. As a result of the defendant's action a

---

[488] *Id.* § 2.02. (2)(b)(I); NY CLS Penal § 15.05 (2) (2003) (New York); § 720 ILCS 5/4-5 (2003) (Illinois).

[489] *See* Commonwealth v. Sama, 411 Mass. 293, 298, 582 N.E.2d 498 (Mass.1991) (holding that "When deliberating as to the third prong of malice, a jury must consider (1) the nature and extent of the defendant's knowledge of the circumstances at the time he acted (subjective component); and (2) whether, in the circumstances known by the defendant, a reasonably prudent person would recognize that the defendant's conduct would create a plain and strong likelihood of death (objective component)); Commonwealth v. Reed, 427 Mass. 100; 691 N.E.2d 560; (Mass.1998) (*Same*). *See also* State v. Sparks, 217 Kan. 204, 209, 535 P.2d 901 (Kan.1975)(stating that "Malice as it relates to murder means knowledge of such circumstances that according to common experience there is a plain and strong likelihood that death will follow the contemplated act.").

[490] Commonwealth v. Pucillo, 427 Mass. 108; 692 N.E.2d 15(Mass.1998) (concluding that "The jury may infer the requisite mental state from defendant's knowledge of the circumstances and subsequent participation in the offense. Inferences drawn by the jury regarding defendant's mental state need only be reasonable and possible and need not be necessary or inescapable..."). State v. Donahue, 197 Kan. 317, 416 P.2d 287 (Kan.1966) (emphasizing that "The existence of malice may be inferred from the circumstances attending the assault, such as the use of a deadly weapon, the character of the assault made, or an unprovoked or deliberately committed attack..."); State v. Dargatz, 228 Kan. 322; 614 P.2d 430(Kan.1980) (concluding that "[I]n a prosecution for murder, the term maliciously has been defined as willfully doing a wrongful act without just cause or excuse...From the factual circumstances, the jury could have concluded that the homicide was committed maliciously by Bo Smith, that is, as a result of the willful doing of a wrongful act without just cause or excuse..."); Swann v.State,412 So.2d 1253 (Ala.1982), *aff'd in* Fears v. State,451 So.2d 385(Ala.1984),(*Same*) Stansbury v.State,218 Md.255,146 A.2d 17(Md. 1956) (holding that "[A]n intent to cause the death of the deceased may be inferred from the character of the assault, the use of a deadly weapon and all other circumstances surrounding the death of the deceased").

[491] State v. Frazier, 339 Mo.966, 98 S.W.2d 707(Mo. 1936).

slight laceration on the side of the mouth resulted, which produced a hemorrhage lasting for ten days and ending in death. The defendant was convicted of manslaughter. The defendant raised two essential questions to the issue of knowledge. Was it an adequate defense that the appellant did not know the deceased was a hemophiliac, and struck only a moderate blow with his fist, which ordinarily would not have been dangerous to life? Is he to be excused because the blow producing the hemorrhage would not have resulted in fatality if the deceased had not been a hemophiliac? The Missouri Supreme Court rejected both arguments, relying on a statute then defining manslaughter as any killing not amounting to murder.[492] As a result, no form of knowledge was ever required for conviction.

The problem lies in the very broad definitions of offenses,[493] which contradict both the explicit directions of the United States Supreme Court[494] and legislature's task of sufficiently clarifying penal statutes.[495] Defining offenses broadly neglects very essential concepts such as the concept of knowledge, which in turn causes unreasonable results. For instance, when the Penal Codes does not explicitly require the knowledge elements, the prosecution does not bear the burden of proving knowledge. Hence, the defendant who is morally innocent because knowledge is lacking or impaired bears the burden of proving his innocence. In so doing, the defendant must plead either mistake or insanity.[496] If he pleads mistake, most of the states require the defendant's mistake to be reasonable to exculpate him.[497] If he pleads insanity, the defendant

[492] *Id.* at 713.

[493] *See* Frank J. Remington, *the Mental Element in Crime-Legislative Problem*, 1952 Wisc. L. Rev. 645, 672 (Professor Remington realized that "[W]ithin the field of homicide we find extremely broad and unrealistic statutory statements of the basis of liability")

[494] *See* United States v. Reese, 92 U.S.214 (1875) (The United States Supreme Court explicitly warned that very broad definitions of the offenses (i.e., Missouri statute), constitute a violation of the separation of powers doctrine.).

[495] *See* Connolly v. General Constr. Co., 269 U.S. 385, 391, Papachristou v. City of Jacksonville , 405 U.S. 156 (1972)(Due Process requires that a penal statute be sufficiently clear and explicit to warn that contemplated conduct is illegal. A statute is "void-for-vagueness" when persons "of common intelligence must necessarily guess at its meaning and differ as to its application…"). *See* People v. Byron, 17 NY2d 64, 67; Matter of Pomeroy v. Whalen, 44 NY2d 992, 994(The test is objective one; a statute is void for vagueness if the reasonable layperson subject to the statute would not know the nature of the conduct prohibited and understand what the law required.).

[496] State v. Snowden 7 Ohio App.3d 358,363, 455 N.E.2d 1058, 1065 (holding that "Mistake of fact can, in appropriate circumstances, negate either knowingly or purposely"). *See* R v. Windle [1952] 2 QB 826; Stapleton v. R (1952) 86 CLR 358 (finding insanity on the basis of lack of knowledge).

[497] *See, e.g.*, People v. Goetz, 68 N.Y.2d 96; 497 N.E.2d 41 (1986 N.Y).

is required to prove that he did not know right from wrong.[498] In either case, omitting the knowledge element relieves the state from proving a basic requirement of guilt, while burdening the defendant with an additional requirement—reasonableness in case of mistake or proving that he did not know right from wrong in case of insanity—to prove his innocence.

Apart from the necessity of the prongs of knowledge to establish liability, the Model Penal Code omitted the requirement of unlawfulness of the conduct that caused death. Normally, the prongs of knowledge do not cause problems in establishing liability in homicide offenses. However, under certain circumstances, requiring the prongs of knowledge exclusively can be problematic. Consider these hypotheses: (a) the police captain who orders his officers to arrest dangerous criminals when it is almost certain that one of the police officers will die in the course of the arrest; (b) the drug manufacturer that markets a product with statistical certainty that a number of people will die;[499] (c) the law enforcement officer who injects poison into the vein of a person sentenced to death.[500] In all these situations there is an implied requirement that is rarely mentioned in homicide statutes that adopted the Model Penal Code. This requirement is the unlawfulness of the killing. In the case of the police captain and the executor of the death penalty, it is quite clear that both enforce the law; therefore, their conducts are lawful. In the case of the drug manufacturer, the license to distribute the drug from the proper authority (the FDA) provides the lawfulness factor of the distribution and thereby negates liability for those who die. If there is no license to distribute the drug, lawfulness vanishes, and the drug manufacturer can be liable for death caused by distributing the drug. In all these situations, the prongs of knowledge are present. Therefore, in the absence of the requirement of unlawfulness and according to the literal application of the law of homicide, the actor in each of the above examples is guilty of a crime.

It should be noted that the requirement of unlawfulness is not a novel requirement. It frequently appeared in the works of the early authorities of common law. Blackstone and Hale considered the unlawfulness requirement as

---

498 Commonwealth v. Rogers 48 Mass. Rep 500 (1844); M'Naghten's Case, 8 Eng. Rep. 718, 722 (1843); Stapleton v. R (1952) 86 CLR 358; MODEL PENAL CODE § 4.01 (Proposed Official Draft 1962).

499 This example was borrowed from Kenneth W. Simons, *Rethinking Mental States*, 72 B.U.L.Rev.463, 473.

500 *Compare* the 13th century analysis of law *in* 2 BRACTON ON THE LAWS AND CUSTOMS OF ENGLAND 340(SAMUEL E. THORNE ed., Harvard University press 1968); he states:

> if it [homicide] is done from love of justice, the judge does not sin in condemning him [the accused] to death, nor in ordering an officer to slay him, nor does an officer sin if when sent by the judge he kills the condemned man. But both sin if they act in this way when proper legal procedures have not been observed...

Id.

the distinguishing factor between excusable homicide by misadventure and involuntary manslaughter.[501] Hawkins suggested that homicide may occur without malice if it happens by an unlawful act or in a sudden quarrel.[502] Stephens concluded that lawfulness arises from the presence of warrant or excuse.[503] Sir Robert Champers conditioned exonerating a defendant upon mistake of fact based on the lawfulness of the defendant's conduct.[504] Correspondingly, American jurisprudence until the nineteenth century regarded unlawfulness as a prerequisite to criminal homicide.[505]

The drafters of the Model Penal Code correctly realized that common law holds the person who was aware of death as a consequence of his conduct as liable as the person who intended it.[506] However, they did not realize the

---

[501] WILLIAM BLACKSTONE, 4 COMMENTARIES ON THE LAWS OF ENGLAND 191(London, A. Strahan 10th ed. 1800) (stating that "involuntary manslaughter, differs also from homicide excusable by misadventure, in this that misadventure always happens in consequences of a lawful act, but this species of manslaughter in consequences of unlawful one…"). *See also* MATHEW HALE, 1 THE HELOTRY OF THE PLEA OF THE CROWN 474(E. Rider, little Britain 1800)(stating " [i]f a man knowing that people are passing along the street throws a stone or shoots an arrow over the house or wall with intent to do hurt to people, and one is thereby slain, this is murder and if it were without such intent, yet it is manslaughter and not barely per infortunium, because the act itself was unlawful: but if a man was tiling an house, and let fall a tile knowingly: and gave warning, and yet a person is killed, this is per infortunium, but if gave no convenient warning it is manslaughter").

[502]WILLIAM HAWKINS, 1 A TREATISE OF THE PLEASE OF THE CROWN (London, S. sweet. 1824) (stating that "[H]omicide against life of another, amounting to felony is either with or without malice. Sect 1. That is without malice is called manslaughter, or sometimes chance-medley, by which we understand such killing as happens either on a sudden quarrel, or in the commission of unlawful act. Without any deliberate intention of doing any mischief…")

[503] JAMES FITZJAMES STEPHEN, 4 NEW COMMENTARIES ON THE LAWS OF ENGLAND 185(London: Butterworth 4th ed. 1903)(emphasizing that "[T]here must be an unlawful killing, the unlawfulness arising from the absence of lawful warrant or excuse").

[504] ROBERT CHAMPERS, 1 A COURSE OF LECTURES ON THE ENGLISH LAW 333 (1767-1773) (Thomas M. Curleyed ed.,).

[505] *See, e.g.*, JAMES M. KERR, A TREATISE ON THE LAW OF HOMICIDE 33(New York and Albany: Banks& Brothers. 1891). *Compare* Coleman v. Smyth, 260 F.2d 518 (4th Cir. 1958), cert. denied, 359 U.S. 946, 79 S. Ct. 726, 3 L. Ed. 2d 679 (1959) (holding that "[T]he omission of "unlawful act" words in an indictment for murder does not constitute a fatal defect").

[506] For further analysis justifying the Model Penal Code proposition *see* Glanville Williams, *The MensRea For Murder: Leave It Alone*, 105 L.Q.R 387,388-390(1989). *See also* Committee of the commonwealth criminal law, Interim Report: Principals of Criminal responsibility and other matters (1991) Para 5.34(The Committee insists that foresight of consequences is different from intention but for the practical purpose of the criminal law they can not be assimilated.) For further analysis opposing the Model Penal Code proposition *see* Lord Goff, The Mental Element In The Crime Of Murder, 104 L.Q.R 30 ,48(1988).

possibility of undesired prosecutions as a result of the literal application of the "knowingly" requirement without the unlawfulness requirement. The only solution to this problem, apart from legislative amendment, is to consider unlawfulness as an implied requirement in the mental state "knowingly."[507]

In sum, in order to convict a person because he knows that the consequence of his conduct is death (i.e., "knowingly" mental state), he must be aware of the nature and the quality of his conduct and the attending circumstances, and additionally his conduct must be unlawful.

IV. INTENTIONAL HOMICIDE WITH AGGRAVATING CIRCUMSTANCES: PREMEDITATION AND DELIBERATION

Typically, deliberation or the requirement of a deliberate act does not cause any definitional difficulties. It denotes an act done in the absence of excitement or passion.[508] Also, it indicates the "cool purpose" or "calm attitude" of the offender while forming his culpable mental state.[509] The deliberation requirement has two notably significant facets. It requires evidential significance to show that the defendant contemplated and desired his actions; and it elevates the grade of homicidal behavior from purely impulsive to completely deliberate.[510]

The terms "aforethought" and "premeditation" are synonymous in that both convey the same notion of "thinking beforehand."[511] Their essence is the time elapsed between forming the homicidal intent and the act of killing.[512] Therefore, proper jury instruction may direct the jury that "premeditation" means "to think beforehand";[513] the jury must find some "appreciable time"[514]

---

[507] *See, e.g.*, State v. Zampich, 205 M 231,667 P2d 955(1983); State v. Patton, 280 M 278,930 P2d 635 (1996)(the courts considered some requirement of liability is essential (*e.g.*, the requirement of "voluntary act"), therefore it is implied, even though it is not expressly required by the legislature.).

[508] Clarke v. State 402S.W. 2d 863,868(Tenn. 1966).

[509] State v. Brown 836 S.W.2d 530,538(Tenn.1992); State v. Speyer, 207 Mo.540, 106 S.W.505 (Mo.1907); Wooten v. State 171 Tenn.362, 103 S.W.2d324 (Tenn.1937).

[510] Herbert Wechsler and Jerome Michael, *A Rational of The Law of Homicide* II, 37 Colum. L. Rev. 1261, 1282-1283(1937).

[511] State v. Jackson, 496 S.W.2d 1,6(Mo.1973).

[512] *See, e.g.*, People v. Barberi, 149 N.Y. 256(N.Y.1896) (holding that deliberation and premeditation imply the capacity at the time to think and reflect, sufficient volition to make a choice, and by the use of these powers, to restrain from doing a wrongful act). *See also* State v. Mathis, 427 S.W.2d 450, 454(Mo.1968) (stating that "malice aforethought" means malice with premeditation; that is, that the unlawful act intentionally done was determined upon before it was executed.).

[513] People v. Morrin, 187 N.W.2d 434, 449 (Mich.Ct.App.1971); Cook v. State, 511 S.W.2d 877,881(Mo.1974).

between the defendant's forming the criminal intent and committing the crime—however, no specific period of time is required.[515]

Deliberation and premeditation usually coexist as a requirement and as a factual consideration. They profile a particular state of mind, specifically, an actor who has sufficient time to *calmly* design to kill. Calmness signifies deliberation, while the elapsed period of time signifies premeditation.

An alternative interpretation of premeditated intentional homicide greatly deviates from the literal meaning of "premeditation" and its significance. Some courts suggest that the term "aforethought," which is synonymous with "premeditation," is meaningless and superfluous, since the requirement is satisfied by the presence of concurrent malice, rather than antecedent malice.[516] This sort of interpretation of "premeditation" or "aforethought" is puzzling for a number of reasons. It challenges our understanding of the early authorities of English common law. Scholars[517] and courts[518] alike requested some degree of

---

[514] Austin v. United States, 382 F.2d 129, 135-136 (D.C. Cir .1967); State v. More, 481 N.W 2d 355,361(Minn.1992) (noting that the "appreciable time" charge is a meaningful way to convey to the jury the core meaning of premeditation and deliberation).

[515] Hickory v. United States 151 U.S. 303(1894); Commonwealth v. Drum 58 Pa 9, 44-45 (1868); Bostic v. United States 94 F.2d 636,639(D.C Cir.1937); Commonwealth of the Virgin Islands v. Lake, 363 F.2d 770,776(3d Cir.1966). *See also* Paul Markus, *Book Review: the Model Penal Code and Commentaries* 73 J. Crim .L. & Criminology 811,819-821(1982) (noting that although premeditation does not require a specific period of time to be formed, it is difficult to see how premeditation can be formed in a matter of seconds.).

[516] Huddleston v. State, 134 Miss. 382, 98 So. 839(Miss. 1924); Campbell v. State, 491 S.W.2d 359, 362(Tenn. 1973).

[517] *See* EDWARDO COKE, 3 THE INSTITUTES OF THE LAWS OF ENGLAND 50(1797) (He states: "Malice *Prepensed* is when one *compasseth* to kill, wound, or beat another, and doth it *Sedato animo*. This said in law to be malice forethought, *prepensed, malitia praecogitata*. This malice so odious in law, as though it be intended against one, it shall be extended towards another.") [*Sedato Animo* means with settled intention; *malitia* signifies wrongdoing; while *praecogitata* indicates that offence was of the most serious class.] *See* LATIN WORDS AND PHRASES FOR LAWYERS 221 (1980). *See also* MICHAEL DALTON COUNTRY JUSTICE 223 (1619) (Dalton concluded that malice must be "antecedent" rather than "concurrent." He stated: "two combat together upon the sudden, and part, and presently after meet and fight again, and the one kills the other; or the one presently fetches a weapon, and comes and kills the other; these seems but manslaughter, for that it is done all in one continuing fury, which was at the first without malice, and could not in so short time be appeased...") *Id. See also* 2 BRACTON, ON THE LAWS AND CUSTOMS OF ENGLAND, PLEAS OF THE CROWN 341 (Samuel E. Thorne ed., Harvard University Press 1968)(Intentional homicide means "By intention as where one in anger or hatred or for the sake of gain, deliberately and in premeditated assault has killed another wickedly and feloniously and in breach of the king's peace...homicide of that kind may be termed murder").

[518] *See* John Royley's case Cro.Jac.296, 79 Eng. Rep.254(1666) (Impulsive intention to kill does not constitute malice). *See also* Hallway's case 79 Eng. Rep. 715 (Where the

settled intention to satisfy the premeditation or aforethought requirement. Moreover, it is very difficult not to recognize a difference in guilt between impulsive killings upon provocation or otherwise—even if does not suffice to reduce the crime of murder to manslaughter—and premeditated killing in which the actor calmly and thoroughly formed his design to kill for gain.[519] Therefore, when the courts overlook the premeditation factor they are, in effect, reducing the minimum degree of guilt required for conviction and equating unjustifiably between two degrees of moral culpability. Ultimately, the court's powers are limited to the application and interpretation the relevant laws. It is never tolerable, after codification of the criminal common law, that the courts override legislative intention by eradicating an explicit requirement by holding that the requirement (i.e., premeditation) is meaningless or superfluous. To do so is to violate the separation of powers doctrine.

Given that premeditation and deliberation are either aggravating circumstances elevating the degree of guilt or an element of the offense, they ought to be proven beyond a reasonable doubt.[520]

In sum, deliberation denotes a desire to kill formed calmly, while premeditation signifies an elapsed period of time between the act of killing and the formation of the desire to kill. There is no reason to suggest that premeditation and deliberation are meaningless or superfluous. They should be proven beyond a reasonable doubt.

V. CONCLUSION

The prongs of knowledge explained in the previous chapter are the foundation of the cognitive state of desire (purposely) and the cognitive states of belief (knowingly and recklessly). They are an indispensable requirement justifying the punishment and a constitutional requirement of Due Process and the proportionality doctrine.

The cognitive state of belief "knowingly" is best explained by the prongs of knowledge. Because knowledge is a matter of degree, the state legislature is free to require any degree of knowledge so long as it reflects the social expectation of justice. A formula for "knowingly" based upon the prongs of knowledge is not perfect unless the "unlawful act" requirement is attached to avoid undesirable/unjust prosecution.

The Model Penal Code's formula of the state of desire "purposely" correctly recognizes the distinction between intention to perform an act that ultimately causes death and purposeful, or desired, killing. The distinction is based upon the notion that intention to perform an act is not a sufficient mental

---

manner of the killing suggests that the defendant's act was deliberate and premeditated malice aforethought is present.).

[519] JAMES FITZJAMES STEPHEN, HISTORY OF THE CRIMINAL LAW OF ENGLAND 84-85 (1883).

[520] *See* Winship, 397 U.S. 358 (1970). *See also Apprendi*, 530 U.S. at 490.

state for liability because it transforms intentional homicide into a strict liability offense, despite its gravity. Thus, an actor is not liable for intentional homicide unless he desires the ultimate purpose of his actions, that is, the death of a person. However, to perfect this formula the foundation must be laid, that is, a number of prongs of knowledge, namely knowledge of the act and knowledge of the circumstances. The actor could not desire the ultimate purpose of his actions unless he was aware of his actions and the relevant circumstances. The difference between "knowingly" and "purposely" is that in "purposely" the actor desired the consequences of his conduct, while in "knowingly" he was merely aware of it.

Deliberation is best understood as a "calm" state of mind as opposed to the impulsive desire to kill. Premeditation denotes the elapsed period of time between the act of killing and the formation of the desire to kill. Usually, deliberation and premeditation coexist to increase the gravity of homicide and to distinguish between hot-blooded, impulsive homicide and calm, cool-headed homicide. The court's failure to realize the rationale of their existence does not justify concluding that either of them is meaningless or superfluous.

VI. PROPOSED JURY INSTRUCTIONS

A. WITH KNOWLEDGE/KNOWINGLY

Proper jury instruction should include the prongs of knowledge and the elements of the unlawful act. The prong of knowledge of the law, or knowledge of the prohibition, is appropriately implied; there is no need to include it in the instructions, since there is a factual impossibility that a person did not know that killing is wrong. Regarding knowledge of the consequences of a conduct, the proposed jury instructions tolerate variations of the degree of knowledge sufficient for conviction.

Proposed instruction for knowingly/with knowledge:

The defendant is accused of committing (name of the offense). You should not convict unless he committed his crime knowingly. "Knowingly" means that the defendant was aware of

1. the nature and quality of his conduct (or appreciated what he was doing); and
2. all circumstances relevant to his crime; and
3. the consequences of his conduct (whether certainty of occurrence, high probability, or mere probability, dependant on the jurisdiction).

Additionally, the defendant's act that caused death was unlawful and the defendant was aware of the unlawfulness. "Unlawful" means that the defendant's act was not authorized by law.

If you find that the defendant was aware of his act, the attending circumstances, and the consequences of his act, and that his act was not authorized by law and he was aware of the unlawfulness of the act, you may convict. If you find that the defendant was not aware of his act, the attending circumstances, or the consequences of his act, or that his act was authorized by law, you should acquit.

B. PURPOSE/PURPOSELY

Proper jury instructions must include the ultimate purpose of the defendant's conducts, that is, to cause death, the knowledge of the act, and the knowledge of the attending circumstances. There is no reason for the state courts to overlook knowledge of the act or knowledge of the circumstances elements in jury instructions. That is especially true when the same courts recognize these elements with respect to "knowingly" and not with respect to "purposely." These courts draw an unjustified distinction, since "knowingly" and "purposely" are both forms of intentional homicide and as such share the same foundations, i.e., the prongs of knowledge. The only distinctive point is that the ultimate purpose of the actor in "purposely" was to cause death, while in "knowingly" he was merely aware of the possibility of death, and death was not his ultimate goal.

Proposed instruction for purposely/with purpose:

The defendant is accused of committing (name of the offense). You should not convict unless he committed his crime purposely. "Purposely" means that

1. the defendant was aware of the nature and quality of his conduct (or appreciated what he was doing);
2. the defendant was aware of all the circumstances relevant to his crime; and
3. the ultimate purpose of the defendant's actions was to cause death to a person.

If you find that the defendant was aware of his act and the circumstances, and that his purpose was to cause death to a person, you may convict. If you find that the defendant was not aware of either his act or the circumstances relevant to the crime, or that his purpose was not to cause death to a person, you should acquit.

C. PREMEDITATION AND DELIBERATION

Proposed jury instruction:

Deliberation is a calm state of mind, as opposed to the impulsive desire to kill. Premeditation requires a period of time between the act of killing and the formation of the desire to kill. No particular period of time is required, so long as the defendant had sufficient time to think beforehand about the crime he was about to commit.

Chapter Five

Negligence

I. INTRODUCTION

No *mens rea* is more controversial than negligence. Commentators are sharply divided upon the suitability of negligence as a culpable mental state.[521] Courts' decisions have demonstrated many inconsistencies in the analysis of negligence.[522] This inconsistency is primarily due to the difficulty in formulating a satisfactorily comprehensible scheme of culpability that shows the negligent actor's actual fault.[523] Two critical theories may play a major role in explaining the negligent actor's actual fault, namely, the theory of knowledge as explained in chapter 3 and the theory of reasonableness as explained in chapter 2. The theory of knowledge demands the negligent actor's awareness of fault, while the theory of reasonableness plays a supplementary role in inferring such awareness. Once the negligent actor's awareness of fault has been established most of the theoretical and moral problems will disappear. Most importantly, the traditional confusion between recklessness and negligence will then be resolved.

It should be noted that awareness of fault may include a number of concepts (e.g., awareness of risk taking, awareness of creating substantial and unjustified risk or, as I will propose, awareness of "failure to fulfill a legal duty").

---

[521] *See, e.g.,* Jerome Hall, *Negligent Behavior Should Be Excluded From Penal Liability*, 63 Colum. L. Rev. 632(1963). *Compare* GLANVILLE WILLIAMS, TEXT BOOK OF CRIMINAL LAW 47(1978).
[522] *See, e.g.,* Moore v. State, 117 So. 2d 469,471(Miss. 1960); State v. Everhart, 231 S.E. 2d 604,606(N.C. 1977); State v. Greene, 348 So. 2d 3, 3-4 (Fla. 1977); State v. Mc Comb, 239 P. 526,529 (Wyo. 1925); People v. Shearer, 9 Cal. App. 3d 74, 78(Cal. 1970); Colo. Rev. Stat. § 18-1-501(3) (2002).
[523] *See* Jerome Hall, *Negligent Behavior Should Be Excluded From Penal Liability*, 63 Colum. L. Rev. 632,643(1963). *See also* MICHAEL MOORE, PLACING BLAME 588(1997); NICOLA LACEY, STATE PUNISHMENT 105-106 (1988).

Part II of this chapter discusses the requirement of awareness of fault as delineated by the early authorities. Part III describes several approaches to negligence. It explains the current theoretical failure of justifying punishment of the negligent offender. Part IV proposes that negligence be understood as "the conscious failure to fulfill a legal duty." Part V summarizes the former analysis. Part VI proposes jury instructions with the suggested approach.

II. THE HISTORY OF THE FAULT ELEMENT IN NEGLIGENCE: AWARENESS OF FAULT

Historically, the maxim *actus non facit reum nisi mens sit rea* (the act itself does not make the actor guilty, unless the mind is guilty), was the cornerstone of criminal liability.[524] Negligence was not an exception to the general rule. The early authorities required some degree of fault in negligence cases. It was typically required that the act that caused death be unlawful[525] in order to convict a person of, in modern terminology, negligent homicide.[526] Foster limited the unlawfulness requirement to *malum in se* (real crime) offenses.[527] Thus, according to this view, to sustain a manslaughter conviction the defendant's act must be a *malum in se* unlawful act rather merely an unlawful act.[528] Foster's proposition implies the fault element in two dimensions: the

---

[524] EDWARDO COKE, 3 INSTITUTES OF THE LAWS OF ENGLAND 107 (1797).

[525] *See* MICHAEL DALTON, COUNTRY JUSTICE 225 (1619) (stating that "[I]f a man be doing of an unlawful act, though without any evil intent, and he happeneth, by chance, to kill a man, this is felony manslaughter and the least, if not murder, in regard the thing he was doing, was unlawful."). *See also* MATHEW HALE, PLEAS OF THE CROWN: A METHODICAL SUMMARY 31 (1678); MICHAEL FOSTER, CROWN LAW 258(1792); EDWARDO COKE, 3 INSTITUTES OF THE LAWS OF ENGLAND 56 (1797); WILLIAM HAWKINS, 1 PLEAS OF THE CROWN 86 (1824).

[526] *See, e.g.*, Robert M. Byrn, *Homicide Under The Proposed New York Penal Code*, 33 Fordham L. Rev. 173, 203(1964)(concluding that early common law authorities recognize only two types of homicide offenses, namely murder and manslaughter. Intentional and quasi-intentional killing (reckless indifference to human life) falls under the category of murder. Other types of homicide offenses, including negligence, fall under the category of manslaughter.) *See also* WILLIAM HOLDSWORTH, 8 A HISTORY OF ENGLISH LAW 437 (stating that "manslaughter is said to be 'an elastic crime' for the degree of guilt which may accompany it extend from the verge of murder to the verge of excludable homicide").

[527] MICHAEL FOSTER, CROWN LAW 258(1792).

[528] *See* Commonwealth v. Adams, 114 Mass. 323,323-323(Mass. 1873) holding:

> It is true that one in the pursuit of an unlawful act may sometimes be punished for another act done without design and by mistake, if the act done was one of which he could have been punished if done willfully. But the act, to be unlawful in this sense, must be an act bad in itself, and done with an evil intent; and the law has always made this distinction that if the act the party was doing was merely *malum*

actor is aware that his conduct is unlawful and that a harmful consequence is foreseeable because the unlawful act is *malum in se.* On the other hand, requiring only the unlawful act, whether *malum in se* or *malum prohibitum*, demonstrates the actor's fault without a qualifying standard of liability. One may interpret the general requirement of unlawfulness to tolerate either a subjective or an objective standard of liability. Consequently, if an objective standard of liability is attached to the unlawfulness requirement, the actor's awareness of the unlawfulness of his conduct is unnecessary to convict him of manslaughter if death was caused by his conduct. This kind of interpretation of the general requirement of unlawfulness would be erroneous for two reasons: the maxim stated above requires a guilty mind and is the governing rule of construction unless there are explicit authorities that require otherwise.[529] This means that the early authorities of common law always required a subjective standard of liability. Secondly, the distinction between the subjective and objective standard of liability did not exist in early common law. Even if it had existed it would have had no practical consequence because every act that causes unlawful harm was presumed to be malicious.[530] Every person was presumed to intend the natural consequences of his conduct.[531] In essence, the law adopted a purely subjective standard of liability in conjunction with a presumption of an objective standard of liability. In other words, the fault element in negligence homicide or the unlawfulness requirement requires some awareness that the act is unlawful; however, awareness is presumed.

In the nineteenth century, courts utilized a number of tests to determine fault in criminal negligence. Some courts decided negligence cases under breach of duty of care theory.[532] Occasionally the courts employed the reasonable person standard in deciding whether the actor materially breached the duty of

---

> *prohibitum,* he shall not be punishable for the act arising from misfortune or mistake; but if *malum in se*, it is otherwise…

Id.

See also State v. Lingman, 97 Utah 180, 91 P.2d 457, 466(Utah.1939); State v. Strobel,304 P.2d 606,618(Mont.1956) (Holding that the "'unlawful act' requirement must be reckless or in marked disregard for the safety of others…it passes the stage of mere *malum prohibitum* and approaches the unsocial aspects of *malum in se*.).

529 *See* Martin R. Gardner, *The Mens Rea Enigma: Observations on the Role of Motive in The Criminal Law Past and Present*, 1993 Utah L. Rev. 635,636(1993) (stating that the maxim by the time of Coke had become well ingrained in the common law, and it remains a central precept of Anglo-American criminal law today).

530 MICHAEL FOSTER, CROWN LAW 225(1792).

531 State v. Vance, 17 Iowa 138, 147 (Iowa.1864); Studstill v. State, 7 Ga. 2, 13(Ga.1849); Darry v. People, 10 N.Y. 120, 137-138(N.Y.1854); Lewis v. Commonwealth, 191 S.W. 2d 416,417(Ky. 1945); Carnes v. Commonwealth, 129 S.W.2d 543,546 (Ky. 1939).

532 State v. Sutton, 10 R.I. 159,163 (1872); Regina v. Carr, 173 Eng. Rep 433(1832); Regina v. Archer, 175, Eng. Rep. 760(1858); Regina v. Johns, 12 Cox's C C 628(1874); Regina v. Campbell, 11 Cox's C C 323,324(1869).

care.[533] Others substituted the unlawfulness requirement with reckless disregard to the value of human life.[534]

The analysis of the history of culpable negligence reveals a number of facts: there is no culpable negligence without some fault element. Initially the fault occurs by performing an unlawful act that then causes death. In the nineteenth century, the courts developed that standard to include recklessness of the consequences and breach of duty of care. Although the law adopted a subjective liability standard, an objective standard was introduced because of the presumption of intending the natural consequences of the act and because any harmful act was presumed malicious. In light of recent Supreme Court decisions regarding presumption of innocence, there is no authoritative power to early jurisprudence regarding the presumption of objective liability, because the law currently neither presumes that the actor intended the natural consequences of his conduct nor that every harmful act is malicious.[535] Accordingly, the only authorities that are soundly valid are those that require that the unlawful act be *malum in se*, which in turn requires some awareness of the fault element.

III. MODERN ANALYSIS OF FAULT IN CULPABLE NEGLIGENCE

A. TWO CONCEPTS BREED SEVERAL APPROACHES: RECKLESSNESS AND BREACH OF DUTY OF CARE

Courts and legislatures developed a number of approaches to express the fault element in criminal negligence. These approaches are founded mainly on two basic concepts, reckless indifference to the consequences of a conduct and deviation from the acceptable standard of care. Courts and legislatures alike utilized these concepts to various degrees to define culpable negligence. One approach required reckless disregard to human life to prove criminal negligence.[536] Others diluted this requirement by requiring mere reckless disregard to the interest of others.[537] A widely accepted approach imported the

---

[533] State v. Hardie, 47 Iowa 647,649(Iowa.1878); *See also* Regina v. Hutchinson, 9 Cox's C C 555, 557(1864) (stating that slight negligence does not suffice, it must be gross deviation from the standard of care).

[534] State v. Vance, 17 Iowa 138, 147 (Iowa. 1864); Studstill v. State, 7 Ga. 2, 13(Ga.1849).

[535] Sandstrom v. Montana, 442 U.S. 510(1979) (stating that the presumption that a person intends the ordinary consequences of his voluntary acts is violative of Fourteenth Amendment Due Process).

[536] Moore v. State, 117 So. 2d 469,471(Miss. 1960); State v. Everhart, 231 S.E. 2d 604,606(N.C. 1977); *see also* Jerome Hall, *Negligent Behavior Should Be Excluded From Penal Liability*, 63 Colum. L. Rev. 632,633(1963).

[537] State v. Greene, 348 So. 2d 3, 3-4 (Fla. 1977) (Reckless indifference or grossly careless disregard of the safety of others is necessary to prove "culpable negligence.");

definition of "civil negligence" in requiring a departure from the expected standards of care to prove culpable negligence. According to this approach, an actor is negligent if he caused harm by his failure to perceive a substantial and unjustified risk, and furthermore such a failure constituted gross deviation from the expected standard of care.[538] The distinctive feature of this approach is the lack of awareness of fault. An actor is held liable for criminal negligence by inadvertently creating risk of which he ought to be aware.[539] Many states lessen the degree of negligence required for conviction by enacting statutes that require ordinary negligence.[540] The concept of a reasonable and prudent person was created to define the expected standard of care.[541] Finally, several jurisdictions introduced a hybrid approach combining the concepts of reckless indifference to the consequences and deviation from the standard of care.[542]

State v. Mc Comb, 239 P. 526,529 (Wyo. 1925); People v. Shearer, 9 Cal. App. 3d 74, 78(Cal. 1970) (noting that "[t]o make an act carelessly performed resulting in death a criminal one, the carelessness must have been gross, implying an indifference to consequences; and the term 'gross negligence' means something more than mere negligence. It means wantonness and disregard of the consequences which may ensue, and indifference to the rights of others that is equivalent to a criminal intent").

538 Colo. Rev. Stat. § 18-1-501(3) (2002); Hawaii Penal Code, HRS § 702-206(4) (2003). *See also* KENNETH W. SIMONS, NEGLIGENCE, *in* RESPONSIBILITY 54 (Ellen Frankel Paul& Fred D. Miller Jr., eds.) (1999).

539 Herbert Wechsler and Jerome Michael, *A Rational of The Law of Homicide*, 37 Colum. L. Rev 701, 1438 (1937). *See also* United States v. Dixon, 419 F. 2d 288,293 (1969).

540 People v. Pryor, 17 Cal. App. 2d 147, 61 P.2d 773 (Cal. 1936); United States v. Henderson, 73 App. D.C. 369, 121 F.2d 75 (D.C.Cir. 1941); State v. Ashton, 175 Kan. 164, 262 P.2d 123 (Kan. 1953); Commonwealth v. Burke, 6 Mass. App. Ct. 697, 383 N.E.2d 76 (Mass. 1978); People v. McMurchy, 249 Mich. 147, 228 N.W. 723 (Mich. 1930); State v. Wojahn, 204 Or. 84, 282 P.2d 675 (Ore.1955); Pehl v. State, 153 Tex. Crim. 553, 223 S.W.2d 238 (Tex. 1949); State v. Munnell, 344 N.W.2d 883(Minn. 1984); Compare, State v. Kays, 492 S.W.2d 752,760(Mo. 1973); Panther v. Hames, 991 F.2d 576,580 (9th Cir. 1993) (holding that criminal negligence is something more than the slight negligence necessary to support a civil action for damages and is negligence of a degree so gross as to be deserving of punishment).

541 Hoard v. State, 95 S.W. 1002, 1003(Ark. 1906) (noting that "[I]f the guilt or innocence of the defendant depends on whether he acted without negligence, or, in other words, without fault or carelessness, then, in order to determine that question, you must compare his conduct with that which you would expect from a man of ordinary prudence and reason under the same circumstances...").

542 *See* Louisiana Penal Code, La. R.S. 14:12 (2003); McLaughlin v. State, 586 So. 2d 267,272(Ala. 1991); Regina v. Bateman (1925) 19 Cr App R 8, 10-12; Regina v. Adomako [1994] 3 All ER 79.

B. JUSTIFYING PUNISHMENT OF THE NEGLIGENT

The mental state of negligence, in any form or shape, encounters several moral and structural problems. The states that defined criminal negligence as reckless indifference to the value of human life unjustifiably equate negligence homicide, the lowest level of culpable homicide, with reckless indifference, which is quasi-intentional and the highest level of culpable homicide. This position is inconsistent with the early authorities of common law, who treated reckless indifference to human life as intentional homicide.[543] Most importantly, the legislature in these states included reckless indifference to human life within the definition of murder while integrating negligence in the definition of manslaughter.[544]Accordingly, when courts define culpable negligence as reckless indifference to human life, the culpable mental state of reckless indifference falls under the definitions of manslaughter and murder. Thus, any prosecution and conviction under the culpable mental states of reckless indifference is based upon the arbitrary selection of penal codes.

In contrast, the courts that define "negligence" as simple recklessness (as distinguished from reckless indifference to human life) render the negligence mental state pointless, redundant, and superfluous, because two distinguishable mental states, recklessness and negligence, become synonymous. This proposition confuses the jury because "negligence" then becomes legal jargon to connote recklessness rather than retaining its natural meaning.

Courts and commentators alike struggled to justify punishing the negligent actor who caused harm by his unawareness of the unjustified risk, though his failure to be aware of such risk constituted gross deviation from the expected standard of care.[545] They faced the difficulty of reconciling the actor's lack of the awareness of fault with the general principles of culpability.

---

[543] *See* WILLIAM BLACKSTONE, 4 COMMENTARIES ON THE LAWS OF ENGLAND 199-200 (1769). *See also* JAMES FITZJAMES STEPHEN, A GENERAL VIEW OF THE CRIMINAL LAW OF ENGLAND 115 (1863); 2 BRACTON ON THE LAWS AND CUSTOMS OF ENGLAND 341(SAMUEL E. THORNE ed., Harvard University press 1968).

[544] *See, e.g.*, Mississippi Criminal Code,

> § 97-3-19. Homicide; murder defined; capital murder.
>
> (1) The killing of a human being without the authority of law by any means or in any manner shall be murder in the following cases:
>
> (a) When done with deliberate design to effect the death of the person killed, or of any human being;
>
> (b) When done in the commission of *an act eminently dangerous to others and evincing a depraved heart, regardless of human life*, although without any premeditated design to effect the death of any particular individual;
>
> § 97-3-47. Homicide; all other killings.
>
> Every other killing of a human being, by the act, procurement, *or culpable negligence* of another, and without authority of law, not provided for in this title, shall be manslaughter.

[545] MODEL PENAL CODE § 2.02(2) (d) (Proposed Official Draft 1962).

The first argument for punishing negligence suggests punishment is not based upon moral culpability, but is intended to educate individuals to be more careful.[546] Therefore the punishment is a way of enforcing rules of prudence in the society.[547] The Model Penal Code adopted this argument, asserting that American courts failed to establish theoretically correct negligence *mens rea*.[548] Proper theory of negligence, the drafters proposed, should take into consideration that punishing the actor who creates inadvertent risk motivates individuals to take care before acting.[549] This motivation generates awareness and thereby is an effective method of control.[550]

This argument might carry some validity if it were supported by data or evidence. According to this argument, the legislature may sacrifice justice in order to endorse a fundamental social objective. However, with no data to support this argument, we would be sacrificing justice for an unfounded presumption. Even if there were data to support this argument, punishing morally innocent individuals for the exclusive purpose of achieving a social objective would generate shock and terror in the society that would outweigh any social benefit.[551] Moreover, this argument does not explain how careful people should be to avoid criminal sanction. If people are required to be excessively careful we will unduly restrain ordinary daily activity.

The contention of the Model Penal Code drafters is that the courts have failed to offer a theoretically correct negligence *mens rea* while formulating negligence in terms of a conduct rather than a particular mental state—which is rather interesting. In purposely, the code describes a state of desire to achieve consequences.[552] In knowingly and recklessly, the code describes a state of belief or foreseeability of consequences.[553] In negligently, the actor is liable not because he formed a particular mental state, whether a state of belief or desire, but because his conduct created inadvertent risk.[554] Basically the code shifts the touchstone of liability from culpable mental states to culpable conduct. The reason for this shift is that the code failed to establish an individual fault element in culpable negligence. Consequently, the code, which largely adopted a

---

[546] Henry M. Hart Jr., *The Aims of The Criminal Law*, 23 Law & Contemp. ProBs., 401, 417(1958). *See also* State v. Wojahn, 282 P.2d 675,702 (Ore.1955); Haxforth v. State, 786 P.2d 580,582 (Ida. 1990); State v. Jacobsen, 477 P.2d 1(Wash.1970) (holding that the negligent homicide statute is a police regulation, and that the legislature did not intend that any form of moral culpability should be an element of the offense).
[547] GLANVILLE WILLIAMS, TEXTBOOK OF CRIMINAL LAW 47(1978).
[548] 2 MODEL PENAL CODE 83 (Official Draft and Revised Comment. 1980) (comment on section 210.4).
[549] 1 MODEL PENAL CODE 243 (Official Draft and Revised Comment. 1980) (comment on section 2.02) (2) (d).
[550] *Id.*
[551] H.L.A. HART, PUNISHMENT AND RESPONSIBILITY 76 (1968).
[552] MODEL PENAL CODE § 2.02(2) (a) (Official Draft and Revised Comment. 1980).
[553] MODEL PENAL CODE § 2.02(2) (b) &(C) (Official Draft and Revised Comment. 1980).
[554] MODEL PENAL CODE § 2.02(2) (d) (Official Draft and Revised Comment. 1980).

subjective liability standard in forming the mental states, has implemented an objective liability standard in negligence. It is fair to say that both implementing an objective standard of liability in negligence and shifting the touchstone of liability from a mental state to a conduct was due to the failure to establish an adequate basis for liability in subjective terms.

To be sure, proposing culpable negligence based on an objective standard of conduct that does not require an awareness of fault is inconsistent with the sprit of the code.[555] The code established a rule of construction requiring that fair warning be given of the conduct that constitutes an offense.[556] The institution of this rule means that no individual should be punished unless at the time of committing the offense he was aware that his conduct was a crime. This rule is virtually impossible to square with the code's negligence formula that negates the awareness of risk creation. It is more puzzling that the code insists on proof of substantial fault in negligence.[557] Does the failure to live up to the hypothetical standard of a reasonable person constitute a substantial fault? Is the lack of individual faculties that make an actor behave in a manner less than what is expected by the objective standard of liability a substantial fault? The code's insistence on the lack of awareness of fault in negligence deviates from the general scheme of culpability that requires such awareness, and makes negligence an odd creation formed to conceal the drafters' failure to establish a satisfactory negligence formula in subjective terms.

The second argument for punishing negligence is commonly called the capacity theory. Under this theory an actor is held liable for negligent conduct if he failed to exercise his capacity to avoid harm.[558] In other words, the actor is negligent if he could have avoided the harm had he taken necessary care by exercising his capacity. Although the actor chooses neither to cause harm nor to perform the prohibited conduct, he had the capacity to choose not to do the harmful conduct.[559] Thus, the capacity theory can be understood in terms of owing a duty of exercising the capacity. Notably, this theory diverges from the traditional requirement of wrongful choice, or the moral blameworthiness doctrine, which required an actual awareness of harm, or at least foresight of the possibility of harm.

This theoretical trend raises a number of concerns. Primarily, the capacity theory demotes the wrongful choice requirement from a fundamental role to a secondary one.[560] The wrongful choice requirement raises the question of moral blameworthiness, which is so firmly rooted in our justice system that

---

[555] 1 MODEL PENAL CODE 240 (Official Draft and Revised Comment. 1980) (stating that negligence is distinguished from purposeful, knowing, or reckless action in that it does not involve a state of awareness).

[556] MODEL PENAL CODE § 1.02(1) (d) (Official Draft and Revised Comment. 1980).

[557] 2 MODEL PENAL CODE 87(Official Draft and Revised Comment. 1980) (comment on section 210.4).

[558] ANDREW ASHWORTH, PRINCIPLES OF CRIMINAL LAW 198(3d ed. 1999).

[559] H.L.A. HART, PUNISHMENT AND RESPONSIBILITY 150-151(1968).

[560] MICHAEL MOORE, PLACING BLAME 589 (1997).

the Supreme Court held it to be an indispensable requirement of the Eighth Amendment.[561] The wrongful choice requirement is virtually incompatible with the capacity theory. How blameworthy is the person who did not know that he was committing a crime? Obviously it is very difficult to hold him liable merely because he has the capacity to know. The situation is different if he knows that he is under a legal obligation to gain some knowledge, and such knowledge would have prevented the harm. However, the capacity theory never suggests that the actor actually knows that he is required to gain particular knowledge. If we suppose the capacity theory is correct, should not the actor have the opportunity to exercise his capacity? To exercise one's capacity, one must know one's legal obligations and thereby have the opportunity to act upon such knowledge.[562] However such very basic knowledge is not required under the capacity theory. Accordingly, even if the capacity theory is correct, it is unworkable given that knowledge of legal obligation is not a requirement of the capacity theory.

It should be noted that knowledge of legal duty/obligation is much broader than mere knowledge of law and includes a number of factors, such as knowledge of a legal duty to act under particular circumstances and knowledge of possible results if the actor fails to act in specific manner.

Ultimately both arguments for justifying punishment of the ignorant actor fail to attribute a personal fault to the actor. This failure stems from the actor's lack of knowledge of his fault at the time of committing the offense.

IV. REDEFINING CULPABLE NEGLIGENCE: INTEGRATING NEGLIGENCE WITHIN THE THEORY OF KNOWLEDGE

Much of chapter 3 was devoted to explaining knowledge as a prerequisite of liability. It was established that knowledge is a fundamental concept justifying punishment, a constitutional necessity of Due Process and the proportionality doctrine, and an indispensable requirement of *mens rea*. Negligence is no exception to the general rule. Some degree of knowledge is required to justify punishment of the negligent. Furthermore, the knowledge element should be implemented in one of the negligence formulas. As explained earlier, negligence is typically defined in terms of recklessness of the consequences or deviation from the standard of care. The approach of recklessness of the consequences ought to be excluded, since it confuses recklessness with negligence. Thus, the

---

[561] Solem v. Helm, 463 U.S. 277, 286 (1983); Coker v. Georgia 433 U.S. 584,598(1977); Weems v. United States, 217 U.S. 349 (1910); O'Neil v. Vermont, 144 U.S. 323, 339-340 (1892).

[562] *See* Jerome Hall, *Negligent Behavior Should Be Excluded From Penal Liability*, 63 Colum. L. Rev. 632,639(1963)(Professor Hall suggested that there is no basis for criminal liability if the actor is unable to use the due care, although he believes that he has the required capacity.).

only available negligence approach is "risk taking through deviation from the standard of care," which was adopted in the Model Penal Code. The knowledge element can be integrated into this approach in terms of knowledge of the legal duty to act or refrain from acting. Accordingly, when the Model Penal Code articulates negligence as "unawareness of risk though the actor should be aware of it," this must be construed as a requirement of knowledge of a legal duty, which in turn requires awareness of risk. For instance, a driver is under a duty not to drink and drive, and not to fall asleep or distract himself by any means while driving. If the driver failed in this duty and thereby caused an injury, he could be negligent because he breached the duty of care, but he must be aware of the duty of care that requires drivers to give their undivided attention to their driving. This kind of legal duty need not be in the form of a law or a regulation because legal duties of care are too numerous to be codified.[563]

For a further explanation of the matter, consider this case. In *People v. Decina*,[564] an epileptic defendant struck and killed a number of children after allegedly suffering a seizure while driving.[565] The court held that knowing a fact that may cause death constitutes negligence.[566] This sort of analysis fails to explain negligence, since knowledge of a fact that may cause harm, or in other words conscious risk taking, is properly classified as recklessness rather than negligence.[567] The defendant could be considered negligent because he consciously failed to fulfill a legal duty. The legal duty is driving safely and the conscious failure is manifested in his awareness of the epilepsy condition, which may prevent safe driving.

Because individuals are required to know their legal duties, reasonableness, or the "reasonable person" rule, can play a major role in determining an individual's knowledge of the legal duty. Therefore, if negligence is phrased as a "conscious failure to fulfill legal duty," then the reasonableness rule suggests that a defendant, as an average, prudent, and reasonable person, should be aware of his legal duties. Reasonableness may be construed in terms of presumption or inference as explained in chapter 2. However, with respect to awareness of the legal duty, reasonableness must be construed as a permissive inference, because considering it as a presumption would unconstitutionally shift the burden of proof of an element of the offense—that is, the awareness of the legal duty—to the defendant.[568] Accordingly, there is a permissive inference of the knowledge of the legal

---

[563] *See* Jeremy Horder, *Gross Negligence And Criminal Culpability*, 47 Univ. of Toronto L. J. 495,519(1997) (stating that "there is no code or rule book by which to judge the performance of those whose behavior is under scrutiny").
[564] People v. Decina, 138 N.E. 2d 799 (N.Y. 1956).
[565] *Id.*
[566] *Id.* at 803-804.
[567] *See* Jerome Hall, *Negligent Behavior Should Be Excluded From Penal Liability*, 63 Colum. L. Rev. 632,633(1963) (Noting that gross negligence has been very frequently interpreted in judicial decisions to mean recklessness.).
[568] *See* Sandstrom v. Montana, 442 U.S. 510 (1979).

duties. Such inference is based upon the fact that the vast majority of individuals, as reasonable and prudent persons, are aware of their legal duties. This is especially true if the legal duties are in the form of statutes or published regulation. Thus, the Model Penal Code's negligence/obligatory awareness of risk (that the actor is unaware of the risk though he should have been aware) might be construed in that form: an actor is unaware of risk though he ought to be aware because of a legal duty requiring such awareness; however, the awareness of the legal duty is to be inferred from the attending circumstances. As explained in chapter 2, construing the rule of reasonableness as an inference will allow the morally innocent actor, who could not conform his conduct to the "reasonable person" standard, to rebut the inference of knowledge of the legal duty and thereby negate negligence.

By integrating the knowledge element into negligence we may realize that the degree of knowledge constitutes a sliding scale that encompasses all unintentional wrongdoing. Initially, we should recognize that negligence is distinguished from recklessness on the basis of knowledge of risk. The actor in recklessness is actually aware of the risk, while the actor in negligence is not aware of the risk though he ought to be because legal duty so requires. Accordingly, a sliding scale of culpability based on state of belief (knowledge) is:

1. Reckless indifference to the value of human life qualifies for murder.
2. Recklessness qualifies for manslaughter.
3. Negligence.

The sliding scale of culpability depends on the degree of knowledge and thereby the degree of blame. In reckless indifference the actor is aware for certain what will occur; therefore his actions should be as culpable as intentional conduct. In recklessness the actor is aware of the possibility of harm; therefore he should be less culpable than the actor who knows for certain what will occur and more culpable than the actor who does not know the possibility of harm. In negligence the actor is unaware of the possibility of harm though he ought to be aware of it because he is under legal duty to know. The blameworthiness stems from the culpable decision not to be aware of the harm even though the actor is aware of a legal duty to acquire such awareness. This actor is less culpable than the reckless one because, although he ought to be aware of harm, he is not aware of it.

Implementing this culpability scheme serves a number of objectives. First and foremost, punishing the negligent on account of "conscious failure to fulfill a legal duty" is justifiable. The fault element and the moral blameworthiness of the actor are established by the actor's conscious decision not to fulfill his duty. In contrast, the existing theories of culpability fail to provide a satisfactory explanation of the moral blameworthiness of the negligent. At best, the existing theories rely upon the legal fiction of reasonableness to determine liability.[569] By doing so, these theories shift the tests of liability from the subjective test of blameworthiness to an external one.[570] This position is difficult to accept because it ignores the lack of blameworthiness of the actor who failed to act at a standard of reasonableness because of his disabilities.[571]

Second, clarifying the negligent actor's subjective fault—that is, that he knowingly failed to fulfill a legal duty—draws a clear distinction between negligence homicide and accidental killing. To draw such a distinction one needs to create a precise test of blameworthiness. Nevertheless, the existing tests of liability in negligence cases utilize unclear external tests of blameworthiness, given that no court has ever given or can give a definition of reasonableness.[572] This imprecision obstructs the jury's fact-finding function, which in turn risks erroneous conviction. In contrast, suggesting that the fault in negligence is a "conscious failure to fulfill a legal duty" clears any past imprecision and thereby improves the fact-finding function. This is especially true in cases that are on the borderline of negligence and accident, in which there is neither a desire to cause harm nor foresight of harm. In these cases, if the jury is left with an imprecise definition of the fault required for a negligence conviction, and the lack of fault required for an accident defense,[573] a considerable margin of erroneous conviction can be expected.

Third, excluding the knowledge element from the negligence definition will result in convicting many morally innocent defendants. For example in *Westrup v. Commonwealth*,[574] the defendant's wife chose to give birth without the aid of physicians. Complications arose and the defendant called for a physician to help the wife.[575] The physician examined the wife over her objections and discovered that she had not expelled the afterbirth.[576] The physician left to retrieve his instruments to remove the afterbirth, but when he returned the wife had already died from hemorrhage.[577] The defendant was convicted for involuntary manslaughter for the wife's death.[578] In the appeal phase, the court reversed the conviction, holding that the defendant could not be

---

569 ROY MORELAND, THE LAW OF HOMICIDE 32(1952).
570 *Id.* at 41
571 *See* Regina v. Ward, 1 All E.R. 565 (1956).
572 *See* Regina v. McCarthy, 2 All E.R. 262, 265 (1954).
573 Goodman v. Commonwealth, 153 Va. 943, 151 S.E. 168 (Va. 1930); Mead v. State, 83 P.2d 404, 410(Okla. 1938); State v. McLaughlin v. State, 586 So. 2d 267,273(Ala. 1991); Edwards v. State, 570 So. 2d 829,831(Ala. 1990);McIvor, 111 A. 616,617(Del .1920); Hunt v. Commonwealth, 289 Ky. 527,530, 159 S. W. 2d 23, 25(Ky. 1942);Wilson v. State, 343 A. 2d 537,540 (Md. 1975);State v. Lovejoy, 357 N.E.2d 424, 428(Ohio. 1976); Ussery v. State 758 P.2d 319 (Okla. 1988).; State v. Brown, 32 S.E.2d 825,828(S.C. 1945); Valentine v. Commonwealth, 48 S.E.2d 264,268(Va.1948).
574 Westrup v. Commonwealth, 93 S.W. 646(Ky. 1906).
575 *Id.*
576 *Id.*
577 *Id.*
578 *Id.*

held responsible for negligence homicide unless he was aware of the condition of his wife that required the fulfillment of his duty of care.[579] If the court of appeal had applied any other test for blameworthiness (e.g., the defendant was not aware but ought to have been aware of the risk) this morally innocent defendant would have gone to jail.

V. CONCLUSION

It is impossible to establish moral blameworthiness of the negligent actor without conscious fault.[580] The history of negligence, the punishment rationales and Due Process, and the proportionality doctrine analysis require knowledge of the fault. Formulating culpable negligence without some degree of knowledge renders the punishment unjustified and unconstitutional. This fact is the driving force behind the proposed culpable negligence approach. Understanding negligence as "conscious failure to fulfill a legal duty" not only solves the problem of knowledge but also offers the jury a comprehensible concept that is easy to apply. Because individuals are required to know their legal duties it is logical to implement the "reasonable person" rule. Reasonableness must be understood as a rule of evidence as opposed to a rule of substance. It raises permissive inference of knowledge of the legal duty. Accordingly, negligence could be formulated as a "conscious failure to fulfill a legal duty," but knowledge could be inferred from the circumstances. The inference of knowledge could be rebutted by contradictory evidence.

A proposed law of negligence might read:

> A person acted negligently with respect to the material element of an offense if he caused harm by creating substantial and unjustified risk. The risk was created because of his conscious failure to fulfill a legal duty. A reasonable person in the defendant's situation would have been aware of his legal duties. The knowledge of the legal duties is to be inferred from the circumstances. The inference of knowledge of the legal duty is subject to rebuttal by contradictory evidence.

VI. PROPOSED JURY INSTRUCTIONS

The defendant is accused of committing (name of the offense). You should not convict unless he committed his crime negligently. Negligently means that

1. the defendant caused the result (death of the victim if the offense charged is negligent homicide) by creating substantial and unjustified risk; and

---

579 *Id.* at 648.

580 See Jerome Hall, *Negligent Behavior Should Be Excluded From Penal Liability*, 63 Colum. L. Rev. 632,635-643(1963). *See also* People v. Angelo, 246 N.Y. 451, 159 N.E. 394, 396-397 (N.Y.1927); State v. Kays, 492 S.W.2d 752,760(Mo. 1973).

2. the risk was a result of the defendant's conscious failure to fulfill a legal duty.

You may infer the knowledge of the legal duty of which a reasonable person in the defendant's situation would be aware. The defendant may rebut the inference of the knowledge of the legal duty by contradictory evidence.

If you find that the defendant caused the result (death) by creating substantial and unjustified risk, and that the risk was a result of his conscious failure to fulfill a legal duty, you may convict.

If you find that

1. the defendant did not cause the result (death); or
2. the risk was not substantial; or
3. the risk was justified; or
4. the defendant was not conscious of the legal duty that caused the risk; or
5. the defendant did not fail to fulfill the legal duty that caused the risk,

you should acquit.

Index

www.ingramcontent.com/pod-product-compliance
Ingram Content Group UK Ltd.
Pitfield, Milton Keynes, MK11 3LW, UK
UKHW041104150926
475561UK00001BA/35

9 780761 828532